Manipulation Secrets

How To Manipulate Anyone In Less Than Five Minutes Using Speed Reading, Ethical Manipulation And Simple Mind Control Techniques

–

Including Case Studies And DIY-Tests

By Patrick Lightman

Manipulation Secrets:

How To Manipulate Anyone In Less Than Five Minutes with Speed Reading, Ethical Manipulation And Simple Mind Control Techniques

Copyright © 2019 by Patrick Lightman

All rights reserved. No part of this book may be reproduced in any form including photocopy, scanning or otherwise without prior permission of the copyright holder.

Do you want to step up your People Analysis Skills and jumpstart your Decision-Making Game?

CLICK here to grab your Behavioral Science Cheat Sheet for FREE NOW.

How To Analyze People
The #1 Analyst Guide To Human Behavior, Body Language, Personality Types And Effectively Reading People

Introduction 7

Chapter 1: Human Psychology Basics Decoded ... 15

Chapter 2: Body Language And Voice Basics Revealed.. 30

Chapter 3: Reading People Through Personality Types 47

Chapter 4: Effectively Analyzing People Through Their Words 76

Chapter 5: Personality And Birth Order 89

Conclusion 99

Dark Psychology Secrets
Learn The Trade's Secret Techniques Of Covert Manipulation, Exploitation, Deception, Hypnotism, Brainwashing, Mind Games And Neurolinguistic Programming

-

Including DIY-Tests

Introduction	102
Chapter 1: Welcome To The Dark Side	107
Chapter 2: Manipulation And Emotional Exploitation	122
Chapter 3: How To Sneakily Get What You Want	141
Chapter 4: Never Buy A Pig In A Poke	158
Chapter 5: Covert Takeovers	185
Chapter 6: Hostile Mind Takeover	218
Chapter 7: Playing Games	235
Conclusion	245

How to Analyze People

The #1 Analyst Guide To Human Behavior, Body Language, Personality Types And Effectively Reading People

Patrick Lightman

Introduction

If I were to ask you, "What is the single most important skill that will give in an edge over others in a personal, professional and social set-up?", what would your answer be? Think about it carefully. We are social creatures and our ability to succeed in life pretty much depends on our ability to understand people. Throughout our lives, a majority of our time is spent in interaction with people (unless you live in a cardboard box or rabbit hole) and developing new associations. If you were to ask me for the single biggest vital survival and success skill in today's world, it would undoubtedly be the art of analyzing people.

How will you figure out if a prospective employee is a perfect fit for your organizational values and goals? How will you determine if the attractive new lady/man you fancy will be a positive and inspiring long-term mate? How will you identify if a potential client is worth doing business with? How will you cut winsome deals with the right business partners and associates?

How will you forge rewarding business connections at networking events? The master key to all of the above lies in your ability to analyze people, identify their personality, recognize how they think and feel, and above all, communicate in a relevant or appropriate manner based on their personality or behavior.

What is it that primarily drives and motivates people? What is the main personality type? What does their body language reveal about their subconscious thoughts? When you learn to analyze people and identify their fundamental personality type and their thought patterns, you can communicate with them in a more effective and meaningful manner.

When you have the ability to analyze people's behavior and personality, you have an edge when it comes to adapting your own words and actions to develop a winsome rapport with the other person, thus forming more productive and fulfilling interpersonal relationships or professional associations. Well, analyzing people isn't just vital for FBI sleuths but also for regular, everyday people to form more beneficial connections.

Learning to analyze people is one of the most effective and sharpest skills one can develop in today's fast-paced world where there is no escaping the importance of forming new connections and constantly interacting with people in a frenzied pace. The power to tune in to obvious and subtle clues people give out all the time will equip you with the superpower to deliver a message more persuasively or convincingly to a person. When you understand how people think and feel, you'll deliver a message in a manner that is suitable for their thought patterns and actions, thus minimizing the chances of misunderstanding.

You will wield greater control over a conversation or enhance your negotiation skills. People who possess the ability to analyze and read others make for more empathetic friends, partners, employers, and leaders. You'll be a razor-sharp businessman and negotiator. As a salesperson or business development person, you'll know exactly what your customer or client wants, which will help boost your sales figures. The scope for conflict-ridden situations will reduce when you understand other people's limitations and structure your communication to suit them.

In short, the skill of reading or analyzing people will determine the quality of relationships you enjoy in life. When you master the tips, techniques, and strategies for reading people, you know what to look for while attempting to understand them. What are the unspoken things that are given away by their body language? What does their choice of words reveal about people's personalities and attitudes? What is their essential character or personality type? How can you tell if someone is telling the truth or resorting to deception? How can you tell if someone is just being themselves or pretending to be something they clearly aren't?

Monthly glossies have done a lot of disservice to the art of analyzing people by reducing it to pop quizzes such as "What your favorite food says about you" or "What does your favorite lipstick shade reveal about your persona?" It isn't as trivial as marketers or glossy editors have us believe. Analyzing people is about delving into people's minds and understanding their words, thoughts, actions, and behavior through psychology-driven principles. It is a comprehensive and deep study that has several factors involved.

Much as you'd like to believe, your favorite fragrance doesn't say much about your personality. It can be highly entertaining and addictive but isn't even remotely accurate. To be a star people analyzer, you need plenty of practice, and the ability to decode personalities.

Though this is a highly intensive field of study involving dynamics of psychology, human behavior, social skills and more, in this book I am packing the most concise, practical and actionable tips that will get you started with reading people.

These techniques can be applied just about anywhere, from your workplace to personal relationships to social life. The sky is the limit when you develop the ability to understand people and influence them using this understanding.

According to research, the ability to analyze people can help us predict the outcome of a negotiation correctly in around 80 percent of all instances. Doesn't that give you an edge when it comes to steering a negotiation in the right direction?

However, let's get started with some valuable fundamental people analyzing rules that will help you set you on the path for being an ace people reader.

Humans are invariably wired throughout primitive times to interact with each other via subconscious signals. Sometimes, people may appear to be happy and content on the face of it, but deep inside their subconscious mind, they may harbor feelings of resentment, frustration and disappointment. When you learn to watch out for these clues, you can reach out to people more effectively.

What is a person's primary instinct or gut feeling? What we refer to as our gut feeling or instinct is nothing but our ability to latch on to specific clues that a person transmits at a subconscious level.

When a person smiles, our smile muscles are reflexively triggered at a more subconscious level. Therefore when someone smiles at us, we smile instinctively in return. Human brains are created to capture clues that are not apparent to the conscious mind. For instance, think about the time when a person was behaving in a pleasant and positive manner, yet you experienced a strong sense of discomfort while dealing with them. This is because our minds are wired to latch on to subconscious signals.

It may be something about the person's body language, including high blood pressure, faster heartbeat, increased palpitations, sweating and more that our mind catches at a more subconscious level that gives us the feeling that something isn't quite right. This explains why sometimes you just don't like some people even when you don't know them well enough to identify their personality.

Chapter 1:
Human Psychology Basics Decoded

If you track the human evolutionary pattern, you will understand that our brains are wired to conduct accurate readings about our thoughts, actions, and behavior. In the absence of language in primitive ages, how did human beings communicate with each other? They communicated through the medium of tone, voice, expression, gestures, postures, signs and other non-verbal mediums. This implies that the skill of reading people already exists within us. It simply needs to be fine-tuned at a conscious level to help us form more productive and fulfilling relationships.

Everyone from trial attorneys to detectives to salespersons to employers can use people analyzing skills to their advantage. Did you know that high-end car salespersons are trained to peep inside their prospective customer's cars to understand their customers better and strike a rapport with them through small talk? If a salesperson sees a golf kit in the back seat of the car, they'll start a conversation about how they enjoy playing golf over the weekends or about a recent golf championship.

Then trial attorneys will attempt to decode where the jury is swinging simply by observing non-verbal clues offered by the jurors while witnesses, officials or the defendant are being cross-examined in the stands. They will also brief their clients about maintaining a body language that generally gives out a positive overall impression about him or her to jurors. This can mean eliminating all non-verbal clues that reveal deception or trickery.

Also, when you learn to analyze people, you view them in a more objective and non-judgmental manner. You will also learn to pick up on clues that reveal deception or untruthful behavior. Let us take an example where people try to manipulate you or get what they want using false flattery. When you master the art of reading people, you will be able to determine if people truly feel those compliments from within or they are simply resorting to fake flattery to get what they want. This helps you protect yourself against other people's vested interests.

Here are some amazing advantages of being a people analyzer:

- You are able to enjoy more fulfilling and rewarding interpersonal relationships, thus reducing the pain of unsuitable relationships. You don't want to kiss a thousand frogs to find that one prince/princess, do you?

- It saves you the time, energy and effort of eliminating toxic people and dealing with only those who match your own objectives, values, and expectations. People who sap your energy can be shown at the door.

- The ability to analyze people can save you tons of money and hours by hiring employees that are the right fit for your organization.

- As a partner or employer, you can tell when people are being deceitful in a relationship or during an interview. You can select a long-term partner who matches not just your own personality but also your values, personality, behavioral traits and more. It will help you weed out dates whose objectives and expectations do not match your own.

- Analyzing people makes you a more power-packed leader. You'll understand your team's goals, motivations, triggers and much more, which can be effectively leveraged for optimizing their performance. This may lead to greater productivity and overall job satisfaction. Learning to read people can be your highway to professional success.

- It is a vital skill when it comes to carrying out negotiations and sales deals. When you figure out how a person prospective client, business associate or customer is thinking, it is simpler to divert the negotiation to your advantage. For instance, if the other party's body language and other non-verbal clues communicate that they are happy with the negotiation terms, yet they ask for a better deal, you know you have to stick your ground because they are simply trying their luck now. Once you realize they are already sold, you won't make any further concessions.

- Reading people helps you fine-tune your own verbal and non-verbal communication for creating a dazzling first impression. It helps you package yourself exactly as you want to create more beneficial connections and relationships. You can position yourself as a genuine, credible, friendly and authoritative individual based on the situation by sending the right verbal and non-verbal clues.

- Your empathy factor increases and you are able to understand people or reach out to them in troubled times more effective to form more productive interpersonal relationships.

- You increase your chances of performing well at job interviews by sending the right verbal and non-verbal signals to recruiters. You know how to create the right impression by communicating the values, characteristics, and ideals that are appropriate for a specific organization or role.

- Tuning in to other people's body language and verbal communication skills makes you an effective speaker. When you gather clues for your audience's body language, you know exactly what they are thinking or feeling about what you're saying. Are they bored, inspired or suspicious about what you are saying? Do they disagree with what you are saying? This will help you quickly change and adapt your speech to evoke a more favorable response. You will be able to say the right things to strike a chord with your audience and persuade them. As a speaker, you'll discover a common ground for connecting with your audience for better results.

- Your chances of electing leaders, politicians, and influencers with the right vision will increase when you learn to understand people's motives through their body language, personality, voice and words. Learn to identify traits that make for a powerful and positive influencer such as integrity, authority, generosity, empathy and more. You will be able to recognize people who truly care about others from those who display vested interests for grabbing power.

People are much like onions. They have multiple personality layers that have to be peeled off to glimpse into their real personality characteristics. Some layers of your personality are apparent, while others are inconspicuous. Sometimes, even we are unable to figure out who we really are because we seem like such a bundle of contradictions to ourselves.

A people analyzer or reader can quickly decipher an individual's personality through several attributes, including what he or she does in their spare time. For example, if you inquire what a person does in their spare time and they reveal they participate in community drives, volunteering activities or contribute to church initiatives, you know they are philanthropic, magnanimous or community conscious. Similarly, if a person says they love partying endlessly or watching television in their free time, they may be low on ambition or seek quick gratification. The point is, even something as seemingly trivial as what a person does in his or her spare time can reveal his or her personality.

Theories of Human Behavior

Classical Conditioning

Classical Conditioning is a popular psychological theory through which people learn by pairing behavior as stimuli and responses to the stimuli. This principle is used for training animals too. Don't you reward your dog with a treat each time it fetches the ball? In the pet's mind, fetching is closely associated with treats or rewards, so it invariably learns that it has to fetch the ball if wants to be rewarded with a treat.

All through our life as human beings, classical conditioning helps shape our behavior. As babies, we come to associate crying with being fed and kept clean. Students learn that studying consistently and dedicatedly gets you good grades. Thus, classical conditioning influences our behavior and acts throughout our lives. We learn to respond to a specific stimulus in a particular manner. It is one of the main factors when it comes to determining an individual's behavior.

Human Behavior and Physiology

According to research, people have peculiar physical reactions to certain stimuli that are valuable when it comes to analyzing them. These principles are usually used in the area of criminal psychology to understand how criminals think and what drives them to commit crimes. With the help of biometric technology, investigators attempt to identify if the suspect's thoughts are in sync with their actions.

This combination of psychological and physiological techniques is powerful for analyzing the underlying motives of human behavior. The human body undergoes specific physiological reactions when a person is misleading or lying. The reaction can be standalone clues or a combination of dilated pupils, an increase in heart rate, greater palpitations, sweating and twitching toes. Physiology or non-verbal clues can help you analyze a person more accurately, though much like other people analyzing theories, it can never be foolproof.

Experiences and Human Behavior

While certain psychologists are of the opinion that our behavior is directly determined by genetics or heredity, others believe that it is a summation of all our experiences since birth. They are of the opinion that our immediate environment or the experiences we undergo in our immediate environment mold our behavior. For example, if a person experiences constant marginalization or prejudice on account of their class or race, they may grow up to despise wealth or seemingly superior races. They may empathize with the oppressed.

Similarly, if a person is constantly bullied, abused or victimized as a child, he or she may grow up to be a bully themselves. Much of their outlook, values, personality, and attitude will be shaped by these early childhood experiences of violence and abuse.

Many psychologists believe that a person is almost always drawn to things they inherently believe they lack to make up for it. For instance, people who are not sure of themselves or don't have a high self-confidence or self-esteem may constantly seek approval from others. They may look for approval and validation all the time.

Have you ever observed people who keenly attempt to read their personality through zodiac signs or astrology? Isn't this a sign of possessing low self-awareness or understanding? People often gravitate towards things they believe they haven't got much of. For example, someone who hasn't been given sufficient attention by their parents during early childhood or teen years may grow up to be a person who thrives on drama and attention-seeking tactics. They may become more dramatic and showy.

There are plenty of clues everywhere. As a people analyzer, you just need to keep an eye out for these subtle clues.

Subconscious Mind and Human Behavior

Our mind is divided into three layers – the conscious mind, subconscious mind, and the unconscious mind. While the conscious mind or state of consciousness is awareness of thoughts, actions, learnings and experiences, the subconscious and unconscious mind are realms of the mind that hold things we may not be aware of. Through the conscious mind, we have an awareness of things we perceive and feel. We can process feelings, thoughts, concepts and ideas that are gathered from our immediate environment.

However, when it comes to the subconscious and unconscious mind, we have little or no awareness of the thoughts, ideas, concepts, and information stored in it. Our conscious mind is only the tip of an iceberg. There are multiple hidden layers, which influence our personality and behavior that we are not aware of.

If you want to be a power-packed people analyzer, begin with yourself. Identify how much you know about yourself or how well you understand your own personality or behavior patterns. Attempt to understand what drives you into behaving in a specific manner. What are your underlying beliefs, fears, motivators, values and more?

Once you've uncovered your own personality and behavioral characteristics, attempt to understand close friends and family members. Lastly, move to strangers who you spot while waiting at a doctor's clinic or at the supermarket/airport or someone you've only just met at a party. Keep practicing to sharpen your people analyzing skills until you are able to read people quickly and effectively, like a pro!

Emotions and Human Behavior

Emotions are brief short conscious experiences that we experience as part of our mental activity. These feelings are not based on rational or logical thoughts. For example, even in the face of compelling proof that our friend is betraying us behind our back, we don't break ties with him or her and prefer to trust them.

As humans, we are prone to acting on impulses rather than logic, reasoning, and evidence. People's behaviors are fundamentally shaped by emotions. Thus, understanding people's emotions gives us the power to comprehend and predict their actions, personality and behavioral patterns.

Chapter 2:
Body Language and Voice Basics Revealed

Do you know that people communicate much more through what they leave unspoken than what they actually say? Body language accounts for around 55 percent of the entire message during the process of communication. In a study conducted by Dr. Albert Mehrabian, it was revealed that only 7 percent of our message is communicated through words, while 38 percent and 55 percent is conveyed through non-verbal elements such as vocal factors and body language, respectively.

Generally, what people say is well-thought and constructed within their conscious minds. This makes it easier to manipulate or fake words for creating the desired impression. Our body language, on the other hand, is guided by more involuntary movements of the subconscious mind. It is near impossible to fake subconsciously driven actions that we aren't even aware of. When you train yourself to look for non-verbal clues, you understand an individual's thoughts, feelings, actions and more at a deeper, subconscious level. Try controlling the thoughts held within your subconscious mind and you'll know what I am saying.

People are perpetually sending subconscious signals and clues while interacting with us, a majority of which we miss because we are conditioned to focus on their words. Since primitive times, humans communicated through the power of gestures, symbols, expressions and more in the absence of coherent language. You have the power to influence and persuade people through the use of body language on a deeply subconscious level since it's so instinctive and reflex driven.

Here are some of the most powerful body language decoding secrets that will help you unlock hidden clues held in the subconscious mind, and read people more effectively.

Establish a Behavior Baseline

Create a baseline for understanding a person's behavior if you want to read him or her more effectively. This is especially true when you are meeting people for the first time, and want to guard against forming inaccurate conclusions about people's behavior. Establishing a baseline guards you against misreading people by making sweeping judgments about their personality, feelings, and behavior.

Establishing a baseline is nothing but determining the baseline personality of an individual based on which you can read the person more effectively rather than making generic readings based on body language. For instance, if a person is more active, fast-thinking and impatient by nature, they will want to get a lot of things done quickly.

They may fidget with their hands or objects, tap their feet or appear restless. If you don't establish a baseline for their behavior, you may mistake their mental energy for nervousness or disinterest, since the clues are almost similar. You would mistakenly believe the person is anxious when he/she is hyperactive.

Observe and tune in to an individual completely to understand their baseline. This helps you examine both verbal and non-verbal clues in a context. How does a person generally react in the given situation? What is their fundamental personality? How do they communicate with other people? What type of words do they generally use? Are they essentially confident or unsure by nature?

When you know how they normally behave, you'll be able to catch a mismatch in their baseline and unusual behavior, which will make the reading even more effective.

Look For a Cluster of Clues

One of the biggest mistakes people make while analyzing others through non-verbal clues is looking for isolated or standalone clues instead of a bunch of clues. Your chances of reading a person accurately increase when you look at several clues that point to a single direction rather than making sweeping conclusions based on isolated clues. For instance, let us say you've read in a book about body language that people who resort to deception or aren't speaking the truth don't look a person directly in the eye.

However, it can also be a sign of being low on confidence or possessing low self-esteem. Similarly, a person may not be looking at your while speaking because he/she is directly facing discomfort causing sunlight. You ignore all other signs that point to the fact that the person is speaking the truth or is confident (a firm handshake, relaxed posture, etc.) and only choose to look at the single clue that he/she isn't maintaining eye contact to inaccurately conclude that the person is lying. Look for at least 3-4 clues to arrive at a conclusion. Don't make sporadic conclusions about how a person is thinking or feeling based on single clues.

For all you know a person may be moving in another direction, not because they aren't interested in what you are speaking about or looking to escape, but because their seat is uncomfortable.

If you think the person is disinterested, look for other clues such as their expressions, gestures, eyes and more to make more accurate conclusions. Include a wider number of nonverbal clues to make the analysis more accurate.

Look at the Context, Setting and Culture

Somebody language clues are universal – think smile or eye contact. These signals more or less mean the same across cultures. However, some non-verbal communication signals may have different connotations across diverse cultures.

For example, being gregarious and expressive is seen as common in Italian culture. People speak loudly, gesticulate with their hands in an animated manner, and are generally more expressive.

However, someone from England may decipher this behavior as massively exaggerated or a sign of nervousness. Enthusiasm, delight, and excitement are expressed in a more subtle manner in England. For the Italian, this retrained behavior may signify disinterest. While the thumbs-up is a gesture of good luck in the west, in certain Middle Eastern cultures it is viewed as rude. If you are doing business with people from across the world, understanding cultural differences before reading people is vital.

Similarly, consider a setting before making sweeping conclusions through non-verbal signs such as body language. For example, a person may display drastically different behavior when he's at work among co-workers, at the bar, and during a job interview. The setting and atmosphere of a job interview may make an otherwise confident person nervous.

Head and Face

People are most likely experiencing a sense of discomfort when they raise or arch their eyebrows. The facial muscles also begin twitching when they are hiding something or lying. These are micro-expressions that are hard to manipulate since they happen in split seconds and are subconscious involuntary actions.

Maintaining eye contact can be a sign of both honesty and intimidation/aggression. On the other hand, constantly shifting your gaze can be a non-verbal clue of deceit.

The adage that one's eyes are a window into their soul is true. People who don't look into your eyes while speaking may not be very trustworthy. Similarly, a shifting gaze can indicate nervousness.

The human eye movements are closely linked with brain regions that perform specific functions. Hence, when we think (depending on what or how we are thinking), our eyes move in a clear direction. For example, when a person is asked for details that he/she is retrieving from memory, their eyes will move in the upper left direction. Similarly, when someone is constructing information (or making up stories) instead of recalling it from memory, their eyes will shift to the upper right direction. The exact opposite is true for left-handed folks. When people try to recall information from memory, their eyes shift to the upper left, whereas when they try to create facts, the eyes move towards the upper left corner. A person who is making fictitious sounds or talking about a conversation that didn't happen, their eyes will move to the lateral left.

When there's an inner dilemma or conflict, a person's eyes will dart towards their left collarbone. This is an indication of an inner dialogue when a person is stuck between two choices. Increased eye movement from one side to another can signal deception. Again, look for a cluster of clues rather than simply analyzing people based on their eye movements.

Expanded pupils or increased blinking is a huge sign of attraction, desire, and lust. A person may also display these clues when they are interested in what you are saying. If a person sizes you up by looking at you in an upward and downward direction, they are most likely considering your potential as a sexual mate or rival. Similarly, looking at a person from head to toe can also be a sign of intimidation or dominance.

When you are observing a person's face, learn to watch out for micro expressions that are a direct involuntary response based on feelings and thoughts. These reactions are so instinctive and happen in microseconds that they are impossible to fake. For example, when a person is lying, their mouth slants for a few microseconds and the eyes slightly roll.

How can you tell apart a genuine smile from a fake one? Pay close attention to the region around the person's eyes. If someone is genuinely happy, their smile invariably reaches their eye and causes the skin around the eyes to crinkle slightly. There are folds around the corner of the person's eyes if they are genuinely happy. Another clear sign of a genuine smile is a crow's feet formation just under the person's eyes. A smile is often used by people to hide their true feelings and emotions. It is near impossible to fake a smile (which is so involuntary and subconscious driven).

Even the direction of a person's chin can reveal a lot about their thoughts or personality. If their chin is jutting out, he/she may be stubborn or obstinate about their stand.

Posture

When a person maintains an upright, well-aligned and relaxed posture, he/she is most likely in control of their thoughts and feelings and is confident/self-assured. Their shoulders don't slouch awkwardly, and the overall posture doesn't sag. On the other hand, a sagging posture can be a sign of low self-esteem or confidence. It can also mean placing yourself below others or subconsciously begging for sympathy.

When a person occupies too much space physically by sitting with their legs apart or broadening their shoulders, they are establishing their dominance or power by occupying more physical space.

Limbs

Pay close attention to people's limb movements when you are reading them. When a person is bored, disinterested, nervous or frustrated, they will fidget with an object or their fingers. Crossing arms is a big signal of being, closed, suspicious, uninspired or in disagreement with what you are saying. The person isn't receptive to what you are speaking about.

If you want to get the person to listen to what you are saying, open them up subconsciously first by changing the topic of conversation. Once they are in a more receptive state of mind, resume the topic.

When a person crosses their arms or legs, they are less likely to absorb or be persuaded by what you say.

A person's handshake can reveal a great deal about what they think about themselves or their equation with the other person. For instance, a weak handshake is a sign of nervousness, low self-esteem, lack of confidence, submissiveness, and uncertainty. Similarly, a crushing handshake can be an indication of dominance or aggressiveness. A firm handshake implies self-confidence and a sense of self-assuredness.

Observe the direction in which a person's feet are pointed. If they are pointed in your direction, it means the person is interested in what you are saying. On the other hand, if they are pointed away from you, the person is looking for an escape route. Feet pointing in your direction or leaning slightly towards you are huge non-verbal signals of attraction.

Legendary Hollywood talent scouting agent once famously uttered, "I don't have a contract with my clients. Just a handshake is enough." You can indeed tell volumes about a person simply through their handshake.

Tone

The tone of a person's voice can communicate a lot about the way a person is feeling or thinking. Look for any inconsistency in a person's tone. Do the tone and pitch vary throughout the conversation? This can be a signal that the person is experiencing a surge of emotions. Listen to the volume of a person's voice. Something may not be quite right if they are speaking in a softer or louder than usual manner. Observe if the person is using filler words rather than concise phrases or sentences. It can be a sign of nervousness or they may be buying time to make up stories.

A person's tone can convey emotions they try to conceal or are unable to express. They may say something flattering to you but their tone may be slightly sarcastic or bitter, which can be a giveaway to what they are truly feeling. It can indicate a more passive-aggressive personality. The meaning of exactly the same words can change drastically when delivered using a different tone, volume and inflection.

Let's say the person ends their sentence on a higher note. Doesn't it sound more like a question than a definitive statement? Similarly, if the person finishes their sentence on a flat note, he/she is making a confident or assured statement. The former can indicate doubt, uncertainty or suspicion, while the latter can be an indication of authority.

Proxemics

Proxemics refers to the physical space maintained during communication between people, which reveals volumes about how they relate to each other. Haven't you experienced a feeling of discomfort when someone tried to invade your personal space or come closer than you appreciate? This person is most likely seeking acceptance from you or trying to make their way into your inner social circle.

On the other hand, if a person comes closer than intended during negotiations, he/she may be trying to intimidate you or subconscious coax you into accepting their conditions. The ideal distance to test a person's comfort level is to stand at a minimum distance of four feet from them. If the person appears open, they are welcoming into their personal space. Similarly, if they are rigid, don't jump into their personal space immediately. They may not be ready to include you in their personal zone.

Mirroring

Mirroring a person's body language is a wonderful way to establish a rapport with a person on a subconscious level. Closely observe a person's body language while they are interacting with you. How is their posture? What are the words they typically use? If they are leaning against the bar or table, follow suit. Similarly, if they sip on their drink, mirror their actions. If you spot them resting their elbow on a table, mirror their action.

Mirroring a person's action gives the other person the impression that you are one among them. It works on a primordial level to create a sense of affiliation, likeliness and belongingness even before spoken language was invented. Adapt your actions, posture, gesture and movements with the other person to give a feeling of "being one among them." If the person is following your actions, they are seeking acceptance or validation from you.

Chapter 3:
Reading People Through Personality Types

Personality analysis is a field that is constantly evolving and varied. There are varying schools of psychological thoughts and theories when it comes to studying an individual's personality. Some of the most popular personality analyzing schools include trait theory, social learning, biological/genetic personality influencer and more.

Personality refers to an individual's distinct characteristics connected to processing thoughts, feelings and emotions that eventually determine their behavior. It involves taking into consideration all the traits a person possesses to understand them as an entity. Personality study also includes understanding the inherent differences existing between people where particular characteristics are concerned.

Here are some of the most common personality type classifications.

Type A, B, C and D

Type A personality people are at a bigger risk of contracting heart diseases since they are known to be more aggressive, competitive, ambitious, short-tempered, impatient, impulsive and hyperactive. Type A personality theory was introduced in the '50s by Meyer Friedman and Ray Rosenman. These people are more stressed due to their constant need to accomplish a lot. They are always striving to be better than others, which invariably leads to greater anxiety and stress.

Type B people are more reflective, balanced, even-tempered, inventive and less competitive by personality. They experience less stress and anxiety, along with staying unaffected by competition or time constraints. A Type B personality person is moderately ambitious and lives more in the present. They have a steadier and more restrained disposition. Type B folks are social, modest, innovative, gentle-mannered, relaxed and low on stress.

Later psychologists came up with other personality types, too, since they found the division into Type A and B more restrictive. They discovered that some people demonstrated a combination of both A and B Type traits. Thus, segregating people into only two distinct personality groups doesn't do justice to the classification. This lead to the creation of even more personality types!

Type C people have a more meticulous eye for detail. They are focused, curious and diplomatic. There tend to put other people's needs before theirs. They are seldom assertive, straightforward and opinionated. This leads to Type C folks developing pent up resentment, frustration, anxiety, and depression. There is a propensity to take everything seriously, which makes them reliable and efficient workers.

This personality type also possesses high analytic skills, logical thinking powers and intelligence. However, they need to develop the knack of learning to be less diplomatic and more assertive. Type C also needs to develop the ability to relax and let their hair down periodically.

Lastly, Type D personality people are known to hold a more pessimistic view of life. They are socially awkward and withdrawn and do not enjoy being in the limelight. They are constantly worried about being rejected by people. Type D people are at a greater risk of suffering from mental illnesses such as depression owing to pessimism, pent up frustration and melancholy. Since the Type D personality doesn't share things easily with others, they suffer internally.

Psychoanalytic Theory

This theory is different from the regular personality classification theories in the sense that the analysis is based is not based on the responses of people about their personality, but a more in-depth study of people's personalities by glimpsing into their subconscious or unconscious mind. Since the analysis is based on a study on a person's subconscious mind, errors and instances of misleading the reader are eliminated.

In psychoanalysis, a person's words and actions are known to be disguised manifestations for their underlying subconscious emotions. The founding father of the psychoanalytic theory was Sigmund Freud, who was of the view that all human behavior is primarily driven by primitive instincts, passions, impulse, and underlying emotions. He theorized that all human behavior is a direct consequence of the equation between our id, ego and superego.

Through the free association method that includes experiences, memories, dreams and more; Freud analyzed underlying emotions, thoughts, and feelings that determine their attitude and behavior. Thus a majority of our behavior can be traced to our early childhood experiences that are still lingering in our subconscious mind, which we may or may not be aware of.

For example, if an individual demonstrates aggressive traits as an adult, it can be pinned down to the violence, harassment or bullying he/she experienced in their early childhood. Similarly, if a child comes from an environment where there were very high expectations from him/her and the parents were seldom happy with his/her accomplishments, he/she may constantly seek validation or acceptance from others. They may fear rejection.

Thus, a person's childhood experiences can help you determine their personality and read them even more effectively according to the psychoanalytic theory. The theory is still extensively used when it comes to helping people cope with depression, anger, stress, panic attacks, aggression, obsessive disorders and much more.

Carl Jung's Personality Classification Theory

Psychologist Carl Jung classified people on the basis of their sociability quotient into introverts and extroverts. Introverts are folks who are primarily inward driven, shy, withdrawn and reticent. They are more focused on their ideas and sensibilities than the external world around them. Introverts are known to be more logical, reflective and sensible by nature. They take time to crawl out of their box and establish a rapport with others.

On the other hand, extroverts are outgoing, friendly, affable, social and gregarious people who live more in the present than worry about the future. They have a more positive and exuberant disposition and are more than willing to accept challenges or changes.

After classifying people as introverts and extroverts, Jung received his share of brickbats from psychologists who believed that the classification was too restrictive to categorize every human being on the planet. Experts argued that a majority of people rarely demonstrated extreme introvert or extrovert tendencies. According to them, only a majority of people possess extreme introvert or extrovert tendencies. Most people, in fact, possess a little bit of both, and their behavior differs according to the situation.

For instance, someone like me enjoys going out and spending time with people but I also value some time alone for reflection and contemplation every now and then. This neither makes me a hardcore extrovert or introvert but more of a combination of both – an ambivert.

Social Learning

This theory talks about how people pick up the personality or behavioral traits from their immediate environment. It proposes that an individual's behavior is a result of their growing up conditions and environment. We pick up specific patterns and personality traits through our experiences. Social learning psychologists are of the view that all our behavior is learned through our social experiences.

For example, if a person has been rewarded in a specific manner, he or she learns behavior through positive reinforcement and experiences. For example, someone throwing excessive tantrums may have learned through their experiences that drama gets them attention. Every time they want attention they know throwing tantrums will do the trick. At times, we don't have to experience something to learn behavior. Our mind is conditioned to use complex codes, information, actions, symbols, and consequences. A majority of our observations and vicarious experiences drive our behavior and help us imbibe specific personality traits.

Ernest Kretschmer's Classification

German psychologist Ernest Kretschmer's personality classification theory theorizes that a person's physical characteristics or personality traits determine the likelihood of a person suffering from mental ailments and their personality.

According to this personality classification, people are classified as Athletic, Pyknic, Dysplastic, and Asthenic. Pyknic personality types are people who are round, stout and short. They demonstrate more extrovert traits such as gregariousness, friendliness and outgoing disposition.

The Aesthetic personality types are people who have a slender and slim appearance. They have a fundamentally introvert personality. These are folks who have strong, athletic and robust bodies and demonstrate more aggressive, enthusiastic and energetic characteristics.

Briggs Myers Personality Indicator

There are multiple personality tests that determine an individual's personality type based on psychological analysis. One of the most widely used personality analysis tests is the Briggs Myers Personality Indicator. It is a comprehensive report that analyzes people's personalities based on how they perceive the world and make decisions.

The Briggs-Myers Personality Indicator was created by Isabel Briggs Myers and Katherine Briggs. It is based on Jung's theory but expounds on it through four primary psychological functions or processes such as sensation, thinking, feeling and intuition.

The MBTI emphasizes on one of the four primary functions dominating over other traits. The personality indicator operates on an assumption that everyone possesses a preference for the manner in which they experience the world around them. These inherent differences emphasize our values, motives, beliefs, and interests, and thus determine an overall personality.

There are around 16 distinct personality types based on this psychological personality analysis theory. The Briggs-Myers test comprises several questions, where test respondents reveal their personality through their answers. This test is also widely used in areas such as determining a person's chances of success in a particular role and compatibility in interpersonal relationships.

In Myers Briggs personality theory, a personality type is determined when there is a clear preference for one style over another. Different letters connected with individual preferences help determine the person's Myers Briggs personality type. For instance, if a person reveals a clear tendency for I, S, T and J, they have the ISTJ personality type.

Extraversion and introversion – The first letter of the Briggs-Myers personality type is related to the direction of one's energy. If a person is externally focused or focused on the external world, they show a preference for extraversion. On the contrary, if the energy is inward-directed, the person shows a clear inclination for introversion.

Sensing and Intuition – The second letter is concerned with processing information. If an individual prefers dealing with information, has clarity, can describe what they see, etc. then they show a distinct preference for sensing. Intuition, on the other hand, is related to intangible ideas and concepts. Intuition is represented by the letter "N."

Thinking and Feeling – The third letter reflects an individual's decision making personality. People who show an inclination for analytic, logical and detached thinking reveal a tendency for thinking over feeling. Similarly, people who show a preference for feeling are more driven by their values or what they believe in.

Judgment and Perception – The last letter of the Briggs-Myer Type Indicator shows a person's way of viewing the world. If an individual reveals a preference for going with the tide and he/she is more flexible in their approach towards responding to things as they arise, they are perception driven. However, if their thoughts are more planned, rigid and clearly structured, they show an inclination for judging (judgment).

1. **INTJ – Introverted, Intuitive, Thinking and Judging**

    The INTJ personality type is primarily inventive, strategic, imaginative, resourceful and creative. They have a clear plan for everything. They are known to be original, analytical, independent thinking and resolute. They are good at planning and executing plans into action. The INTJ personality type is perceptive when it comes to recognizing patterns and giving a clear logical reason for patterns.

    They have a high sense of responsibility and commitment and rarely quit something without completing it. They have high expectations not just from themselves but others too. The INTJ personality type makes for wonderful leaders and also dedicated followers. These are generally the kind of people you want as original and independent thinking leaders.

2. ISTJ – Introverted, Sensing, Thinking, Judging

ISTJs are composed, quiet, reserved, serious and contemplative. They are primarily focused on living a secure, unruffled and peaceful life. These people are highly reliable, meticulous, disciplined, responsible and precision-oriented. They are logical, rational and practical. ISTJ folks possess a steady approach when it comes to fulfilling their objectives.

There is a deep respect for position, authority, establishment and a more conventional way of living. ISTJ people are concerned about maintaining order in their immediate physical space, work, and life. If you are looking for administrators or managers for your business, these people may be a good fit.

3. ISFJ – Introverted, Sensing, Feeling, Judging

ISFJ people are quiet, kind, responsible conscientious. They are focused on fulfilling their responsibilities and obligations. There is a clear tendency for being practical, balanced and steady. They have an inherent need to place the feelings and needs of other people over theirs. ISFJ personality type people lean towards conventions and established norms. They don't believe in challenging customers and are more concerned about leading a peaceful and secure life.

The ISFJ personality type is intuitively tuned in to the needs, emotions, and feelings of other people. They have a deep service sense and are suitable for vocations where they are needed to be of help to other people.

4. ESTJ – Extroverted, Sensing, Thinking and Judging

ESTJ people live in the moment and have a high sense of appreciation for the present moment. They demonstrate a high sense of reverence for conventions, traditions and established customs, and they'll rarely go against it. ESTJ folks have a good idea about how things should be resolved speedily and effectively. This makes them a good fit for leadership positions. They are logical, rational, practical and innately realistic.

The ESTJ personality type excels at managing complex projects and is focused on completing things with careful attention to details. They are reliable and dependable when it comes to accomplishing challenging tasks. The ESTJ personality type put in a lot into each task they undertake, which makes them efficient project managers or leaders. They place a lot of premium on law, justice, social order and security.

5. ISTP – Introverted, Sensing, Thinking and Perceiving

ISTP type people are inquisitive, curious and intelligent people who are always focused on knowing how everything works. They demonstrate a composed, peaceful and unruffled disposition. ISTP people also possess highly developed motor/mechanical skills and show an inclination for an intense adventure. These people are more tolerant, flexible and adaptive by nature. They are excellent observers, people watchers and analyzers. ISTP folks are known to dive into the base of any situation before they come up with an actionable solution.

They will almost always emphasize organizing facts, and establishing a precise cause and effect relationship. These are almost always the problem solvers, analyzers or solution providers that appear more logical and emotionally detached. Their solutions are more logically driven and less determined by emotions.

6. ISFP – Introverted, Sensing, Feeling, Perceiving

ISFP personality type people are shy, reflective, kind and sensitive. They avoid confrontation, arguments or heated conflict, and always focus on forming peaceful and harmonious relationships. ISFP people will avoid situations where there is scope for conflict. One distinct characteristic is the ISFP type's evolved sense of aesthetics. There is a higher tendency to be broadminded, adaptive and accommodating.

The ISFP folks aren't obstinate about their views and posses a high sense of balance and appreciation for other people's views. They will agree to disagree with others in a graceful manner. ISFP type people are inventive, independent thinking and path-breaking original. They safeguard their space fiercely and attempt to work within the given time frame with diligence. They live for the moment and aren't too worked up about their future.

7. ESTP – Extroverted, Sensing, Thinking, Perceiving

ESTP personalities are outgoing folks who use a more rational, practical and logical approach while handling challenges. They focus on gaining fast results and solutions. ESTP people very efficient when it comes to analyzing people through multiple clues! They make for excellent psychologists, investigators and people analyzers. They are intuitive and pick on both verbal and non-verbal clues effectively.

The ESTP personality type is action-oriented and practical and prefers tangible actions over intangible ideas. They have a more problem solving, energetic, enthusiastic and proactive approach to life. They ESTP type people are more spontaneous, focused, random and attentive. Their ideal learning approach is hands-on knowledge or learning by doing. They seek solutions by actively taking their problems head-on.

8. ESFP – Extroverted, Sensing, Feeling, Perceiving

ESTP type people are gregarious, flexible, amiable, loving and contemplative by nature. They seek new experiences, alternatives, and possibilities. This personality type is also open to figuring out new ways to do things. They also like unique, unusual and off-beat stuff. These people are high on positivity and optimism.

They also make for exceptionally good team members and love to combine their skills with other people to accomplish great results. These are folks who believe in living life queen or king size, while also developing solid relationships with others. The ESFP type is not very good when it comes to handling expectations, pressure and stress. They become pessimistic, negative and insecure.

9. ENTJ – Extroverted, Intuitive, Thinking and Judging

The ENTJ personality type is forthright, straightforward and outspoken, which makes them excellent leaders. According to them, the world is full of possibilities. Rather than perceiving problems as hurdles, they view them as challenges. ENTJ personality type people are ambitious, practical, career-minded and solution-oriented.

They will consider problems from several angles before coming up with practical, effective and workable solutions. The ENTJ personality type is in its element when it comes to goal setting and fulfilling these goals. The ENTJ personality types are outspoken, clear decision-makers and effortless leaders. For these people, the world is full of possibilities.

They are well-read, knowledgeable, abreast of what is happening in the world and more aggressive when it comes to expressing their ideas. While they may not be too intuitively connected to other people's feelings, ENTJs can be surprisingly emotional.

10. INFP – Introverted, Intuitive, Feeling and Perceiving

The INFP personality type folks are balanced, composed, calm and contemplative. They are fiercely loyal and true to their value system. These people care deeply about others. They have a strong belief and value system, which guides them while making important decisions. The INFP people are loyal, adjusting, reliable, adaptable to change and relaxed. They easily empathize with other people and reach to other people to make things easier for them.

11. INTP – Introvert, Intuitive, Thinking, Perceiving

INTP type people are independent thinking, creative, logical and analytic. They have a high sense of respect for knowledge and skills. By nature, they are reserved, reticent and withdrawn. They tend to exist in a world of their own and show little inclination for following others. The INTP personality type is fiercely independent and individualistic. They believe in creating their own route rather than following the one set by others.

12. **ENFJ – Extroverted, Intuitive, Feeling and Judging**

The ENFJ people have inherently well-developed people skills and are known to be empathetic, kind, disciplined and affectionate. They are more externally focused and seldom enjoy being by themselves. The ENFJ people demonstrate an exceptional ability for spotting talent and skills in people. They also go out of the way to help people fulfill their real potential, thus making them wonderful leaders and managers.

One of the ENFJ personality type's best trait is their ability to accept praise and criticism with equal ease while being faithful to people.

13. ESFJ – Extroverted, Sensing, Feeling and Judging

ESFJ personalities are people who thrive when they are in the midst of other people. They are people persons, who enjoy interacting with other people, developing meaningful relationships with them, and getting to know them well. There is a huge need to be liked, admired and accepted by others. The ESFJ personality type desires that everything around them should be positive, balanced and harmonious for which they may go all out to support other people.

ESFJ people possess an inherent knack when it comes to making other people feel good about themselves. They will compliment and praise people lavishly in public, and ensure their strengths are highlighted. This personality type is popular because they have an inherent ability to make others feel special.

Their value or belief system is primarily guided by people around them, which makes them less rigid when it comes to their value system and beliefs. Also, they are more flexible when it comes to different situations and persons. The ESFJ types enjoy being appreciated and are in their element when it comes to contributing to mankind's welfare. In any situation, they are concerned about the greater good.

14. ENTP – Extroverted, Intuitive, Thinking and Perceiving

The ENTP personality type is excited by ideas and concepts. They are able to analyze people and situations instinctively. They are fast decision-makers and action takers. ENTP type people are also more alert, guarded, forthright and attentive. They are more fixated on possibilities or alternatives than plans.

They are excellent conversationalists who leave everyone bewitched with their words. ENTP doesn't like sticking to a routine and is constantly seeking new experiences. They are experts at reading people and have a deep sense of respect for learning. Again, they will consider multiple possibilities before zeroing down on a single solution.

15. ENFP – Extroverted, Intuitive, Feeling and Perceiving

The ENFP personality type people are fiercely independent, original and individualistic by nature. They believe in creating their own unique methods, habits, ideas, concepts, and actions. This personality type doesn't fancy interacting with cookie clutter folks who follow the herd. They also despise being constrained in a box.

The ENFP personality type enjoys being around others and possesses a strong sense of intuitive and sensitivity for others as well as themselves.

They are more driven by emotions and are known to be perceptive and contemplative. The ENFP personality type will think deeply about things from an emotional perspective before making a decision.

ENFP people are capable of accomplishing success in tasks that interest them. However, they also have a tendency to get easily bored doing things they aren't really good at. They don't fare too well when it comes to jobs that involve more meticulous, routine and detail-oriented tasks. They thrive in professions that allow them to express their creativity and come up with innovative ideas. Positions that are more confining and boxed will not appeal to them.

16. INFJ – Introverted, Intuitive, Feeling and Judging

INFJ personality types are idealists, observers and visionaries who thrive on ideas and imagination. They have a unique and profound way of viewing the world. This personality type has the tendency to look at the world in a substantial and in-depth manner. They will seldom accept things as they are. While others view the INFJ personality as weird or eccentric, they stick to their unusual views about life.

The INFJ people are compassionate, caring, gentle and complex individuals who are more inclined towards creative, independent and artistic endeavors. They reside in a world that filled esoteric possibilities. While this personality type places a high premium of order and organization, they can also be surprisingly spontaneous and intuitive.

They will be able to understand ideas intuitively without pinpointing the reason. This makes the INFJ people less organized and systematic than other judging personality types.

Chapter 4:
Effectively Analyzing People Through Their Words

We don't use words mindlessly. There is a reason (often subconscious) behind our choice of words. The words we use are often guided by our subconscious feelings, emotions, and thoughts. There is a clear underlying meaning behind phrases, words and other verbal expressions. Let us say for example, a person tells you that "Oh, so now you are dating another doctor." What does their choice of the word "another" indicate? It may imply that you just got out of a terrible relationship with a doctor, and foolhardily started dating another.

People use "yeah" and other similar terms when they want to communicate ambivalence. Similarly, they use "dude", "sis" or "bro" to express solidarity with people. It can be a sign of loyalty or friendship. There may also be a deep-seated need to be liked or accepted by the other person. People using these terms may seek to establish a sense of familiarity and belongingness with others. Begin by closely observing people's words and use them for peeking into the mind to unveil the thoughts and emotions behind their expressions.

Watch Out For Adjectives and Adverbs

The human brain is no short of a marvel. It is incredibly effective when it comes to thinking and vocalizing thoughts and/or ideas. When we think, our brains primarily use verbs and nouns. However, when we convert ideas or thoughts into language, we tend to elaborate on our thoughts by using adverbs and adjectives. These adverbs and adjectives that we use for describing basic nouns and verbs can reveal a lot about our inner feelings, thoughts, and emotions. They can also offer a glimpse into our predominant values, and other ideas.

For example, let us consider a sentence such as "I ate". It comprises a pronoun and an action verb. The words or expressions used to modify these sentences can offer plenty of information about a person. These are modifying words that give clues into an individual's value system or behavioral patterns. Through verbal expressions or clues, you can make a fairly reliable guess about an individual's state of mind or character. If you add "fast" to the above sentence, it indicates urgency.

They may eat fast because they are late for a meeting or are conscious of being punctual. It can reveal a more commitment-driven, responsible, dedicated and disciplined approach. They have a deep sense of respect for social norms and may be focused on other's expectations. They may be your ideal employees since they are fast, punctual and committed. Of course, there can be plenty of other reasons why a person eats fast. However, descriptive words can offer you a good indication of people's thoughts, behavior and overall values.

Read Between the Lines

Not everything people say reveals a lot about them. Often, what they leave unsaid also says a lot about them. Even when someone offers you a compliment such as "You are looking cool today", it may not go down well with you. To you, it may imply that you are looking cool only today and not every day. We subconsciously tune in to what is left unsaid.

Let us take another example to understand the hidden meaning behind words or what people leave unsaid. You take your friends out on a newly opened restaurant in your neighborhood. It's a much talked about place and you just can't wait to try the stuff there. As soon as you enter, the waiter/server greets you warmly and directs your group to the table.

What follows is an elaborate seven-course meal. Before serving you each of the scrumptious courses, the waiter introduces each course and tells you interesting details about the preparations. You have a great time wining and dining with friends. Once you finish the entire seven-course meal, you request the waiter to bring your check.

The waiter brings over your check and asks you for your feedback about the food. You sum it up in a single line by stating, "The soup was good." The waiter doesn't react too positively and looks a tad disappointed. You wonder why! According to you, you just paid him/her a compliment. However, the things you left unsaid revealed a lot about your opinion or thoughts regarding the food.

The other person subconsciously latched on to what you left unsaid. It revealed that apart from the soup, nothing else was worth mentioning or everything other than the soup was average. While people communicate plenty through what they say, they leave a lot of things unsaid.

I Test

This is yet another verbal determinant of an individual's personality. If a person uses the term "I" excessively, it indicates self-centeredness, selfishness or a large ego. However, the more "I" a person uses, the less powerful he/she feels. People who aren't sure about their power feel the desire to establish a false sense of power through excessive usage of "I." Do a tiny exercise right now. Browse through the mails that are sent by people in a position of high authority. Now compare these mails will people who aren't in very authoritative positions, you'll clearly notice more usage of "I" in the latter.

For example, "Dear Jones, I was a student in your biology class last year. I have always enjoyed being a part of your classes. I've learned a lot through them. I received an email from you related to research collaboration. I would really appreciate working with you." Mr. Jones may reply with "That's amazing news. This week may be slightly busy for me due to prior commitments. How about a meeting next Tuesday from 5 to 7? It will be wonderful to catch up."

Other than an indication of less power and higher self-consciousness, it is also a clue of depression. Research published in Scientific Study of Literature revealed that illustrious poets who committed suicide frequently resorted to the usage of first-person pronouns while writing poetry.

Talking About Others

What people say about other people is often a reflection of their own personality. In a research conducted by Siminie Vazire and Peter Harms, it has been discovered that asking people to rate others on three negative and three positive aspects gave plenty of insights about their social personality, overall being, mental health and their view about others. It was found that a person's tendency to see others in a more positive light indicates their own positivity.

There is a powerful link between having an opinion about other people and possessing an energetic, courteous, optimistic, emotionally balanced and kind personality. Talking positively about other people demonstrates how positively they view their own lives. On the other hand, people who use unflattering and negative words and phrases view themselves in an inferior light.

There is a greater correlation between using unflattering words used for describing other people and narcissism, low self-confidence, anti-social tendencies, frustration, overall dissatisfaction and more. People with a primarily negative personality type tend to view others in a more unflattering light. This can be a strong indication of mental issues, personality disorder or an unstable mind.

The Object Description Analysis

The manner in which a person describes an object is also enough to give you a fair idea about how the individual views the world, along with how he/she thinks and feels. The most commonly used cluster words will offer a clear basis for their behavior and personality. This linguistic personality determination technique is called meaning extraction.

Additional Words

The extra or additional words a person uses while conversing with you can reveal a lot about their thoughts, behavior, and personality. For example, if someone says, "I won yet another award" in place of "I won an award", it reveals a need to tell people that they've won plenty of awards earlier. The individual may be struck with a terrible complex that makes them scream about their objection from rooftops.

Pick up this clue and learn that one of the best ways to develop a rapport with this person is to hail them for their accomplishments. Their words present an area of weakness that you can quickly cash on. Watch out for incompatibility between the person's verbal and non-verbal clues. For example, an individual may state that they are delighted to meet you. However, if their body language is rigid, inflexible and uncomfortable, something may be wrong. A trained eye can easily figure out inconsistencies between a person's verbal and non-verbal signals.

You can fall back on their words and body language collectively to understand what the person is thinking or feeling.

"I Made Up My Mind" – Introverts and Extroverts

If an individual says he/she has made up their mind, they have most likely considered several options before making a clear decision. It implies that a person is prone to contemplating and reflecting upon their decision rather than making spur of the moment decisions. They have deliberated on their decision and maybe analytic or logical by nature.

There are lesser chances of them being rash, spontaneous and impulsive decision-makers. The words are an indication of a person's introvertedness and extrovertedness. Taking decisions after giving it a thought is a sign of introvertedness.

However, guard against making instant, sporadic decisions about people based on the words they use. Simply using "decided" or "I made up my mind" isn't enough to make conclusions about an individual's personality. Identify a clear pattern and several verbal/non-verbal clues to read people more effectively. Watch out for clues that support your initial reading or point to contrary evidence.

Extroverts collect their energies from other people and their environment. The stimulation and decision making comes from using the trial and error technique over reflectively contemplating their decision. Extroverts may speak more spontaneously without thinking, while introverts will carefully weight their words and their implications.

You can tailor your own communication pattern to suit the other person's once you get to know if they are an introvert or extrovert. Identifying whether a person is an introvert or extrovert helps you understand how someone makes decisions. For example, let us say you are selling insurance. You may have to determine what drives both the introvert and extrovert personality types to make a decision about buying insurance.

Introverts may be more reflective and mull over the options before making a decision, while extroverts are more prone to making quick decisions. If you notice a primarily introverted mindset, give people more time to think before making a decision. Pushing these folks to make a quick decision may backfire. They may get uncomfortable with the idea of being pushed into a decision.

If you are negotiating important business deals, you don't give introverts enough time to mull over the conditions, they may come up with a negative response. On the contrary, people who make fast decisions show signs of being extroverts. They can be pushed into making fast decisions. However, one of the most vital things to keep in mind is that people rarely demonstrate absolute introvert or extrovert tendencies. A majority of people are a combination of introvertedness and extrovertedness.

Chapter 5:
Personality And Birth Order

An individual's birth order can also reveal a lot of his or her personality. This isn't just restricted to pop psychology talk or mindless party chatter but based on a psychological analysis of how the person relates to their family members and how they are treated within the family based on their position or birth order. A person's family dynamics play a considerable role in shaping their personality. The role they fulfilled as children or during their adolescent years influences their behavior as adults. Our status quo as children establishes the foundation for our actions as adults. Notice how several times children born in the same family or raised in the same environment have dramatically diverse personalities.

Of course, there are other factors that in combination with a person's birth order can determine their personality type. These factors such as the family's overall socio-economic status, education, number of children in the family, parent's professional achievements and more also impacts an individual's personality.

It was Alfred Adler who first came up with the theory of studying an individual's personality through their birth rank. He used it as a method for reading the behavior, personality and actions of his clients. However, it was Frank Sulloway who elaborated on the theory in his publication *Born to Rebel*. Sulloway's book identified five primary traits like extraversion, agreeableness, neuroticism, consciousness and openness.

The psychologist mentioned that an individual's birth order impacts their personality even more than their environment. This means that the chances of two first-borns having the same personality type are higher than two children belonging to one family.

Here are some ways to read a person through their birth order.

First-borns

Firstborn children are known to be responsible and ambitious leaders, who pave the way for others. They are original, creative and independent thinking by nature. Since they get more undivided attention and time with their parents, they have a clear edge over their siblings. Again, they are more proactive and take the lead when it comes to caring for the siblings, which makes them more disciplined, inspiring, responsible and accountable as adults. They are protective towards those weaker than them, and often lead others.

If parents place a lot of expectations on the first in a household, the person may grow up feeling inadequate. This may not just lead to low self-esteem but also a weak personality that is marked by a constant need for validation, acceptance and approval. The person may end up feeling that they can never be good enough for anything.

Firstborn individuals are more goal-oriented and ambitious. They give plenty of importance to accomplishments and success. They thrive in or perform well in positions of authority, responsibility and maintaining discipline. There is an inherent tendency to be a control freak, while also being autocratic, dictatorial and bossy.

Owing to the fact that come first in the sibling hierarchy, these people are physically stronger than other children in the household, which gives them a marked dominant personality. They may have a high sense of entitlement.

First-borns are often high on determination, rule enforcement and attention to details.

Middle-borns

Since they are caught between two siblings, middle-borns develop a more complicated personality. They are neither given the rights and responsibilities of the older sibling nor the special privileges of the youngest sibling. This makes them look outside the home for friendships and connections.

Middle-borns often have very big social circles and are known to be excellent diplomats and negotiators. They are social creatures who function with a profound sense of peace and fairness. Middle-borns are fiercely loyal to their loved ones and seldom betray people's trust. Typical personality traits of middle born children are flexibility, generosity and adaptability. They are known for their diplomatic nature and can play peacemakers in any situation.

Middle born children are primarily understanding, co-operative and adjusting. They also turn out to be competitive adults. Middle-borns have a close-knit social circle who award them the affection they haven't received within their family. Middle-borns are late raisers and discover their calling after plenty of experimentation, contemplation and deliberation. They are at the center of authoritative careers that allow them to utilize their power-packed negotiation skills.

Middle-borns are generally social and operate with a deep sense of justice and fairness. Their typical personality characteristics include generosity, diplomacy, flexibility, and adaptability. They are good at teamwork and relate well with people belonging to multiple personality types since they have learned to deal with older and younger siblings. Middle-borns display a more affable nature, and they know how to wriggle themselves out of confrontations and conflicts. They are known to be resourceful and quickly master multiple skills.

Last Born

By the time the youngest child of the family is born, parents are well-versed in their parenting skills and more economically settled. This makes them less paranoid and more secure. They aren't excessively monitored, which makes them more independent and freedom. Last borns are excellent decision-makers and operate with a high sense of entitlement.

The last born is known to be charming and risk-taking. They are independent thinking, original and adventurous. There is a greater tendency to rewrite the rules rather than following set norms.

Parents are less careful when it comes to their last born because they've already experienced being a parent, which helps them give more leeway and flexibility to the youngest child. Also, there are higher chances of pampering and indulging the child owing to a better financial status. Since parents are more relaxed and lenient with last-borns, they don't turn out to be conformists. They are used to plenty of attention, and they don't worship authority.

Rather than walking on set paths, they will create their own path. Since they've learned to compete with their siblings for their parent's time and attention, they are good are handling competition and aren't easily bothered by feelings of envy and insecurity.

Since they are more creative and independent thinking, they thrive in careers such as stand up comedians, painters, dancers, and authors. Typical personality characteristics include empathy, obstinacy, extroversion, manipulativeness, a penchant for drama and more. These are your salespeople since they are glib and can talk themselves of almost any situation.

Sole Child

The only child doesn't have to compete with anyone for their parents' time and attention, which makes them self-centered. There is a tendency to think that everything revolves around them. They tend to spend a lot of time alone, which turns them into more original, resourceful, inventive and creative people. Sole or only children find new and innovative ways to keep themselves busy. By nature, they are more confident, self-assured, meticulous, expressive and firm. They express their opinions more assertively and confidently.

Since they do not have to deal with sibling rivalry of any kind, they are always used to having things their way. They become edgy and unsettled when they have to compete with others or things don't go their way. Sole-borns find it tough to share the limelight with others. They almost always want to be the center of attention since they've never had to complete with any attention at home through their childhood and adolescent years. Only-borns are constantly seeking attention, respect and attention. In the absence of siblings as role models, their only role models are elders of the house. Since grown-ups become their role models, they grow up to be perfectionists.

There are multiple factors that impact a person's behavioral characteristics and personality. To make a more accurate reading of an individual's personality through birth order, there are some effective tips offers by psychologists. They recommend analyzing a person's siblings while reading their personality since no two children in the same household ever share the same role. If one assumes the role of a caretaker, the other will invariably be the care recipient.

Another factor that is taken into consideration while analyzing an individual's personality through birth order is genetics, gender, social status and other factors (apart from their birth order). These factors together will help you make more accurate readings about an individual's personality than simply relying on birth order.

Conclusion

I genuinely hope this book has offered you multiple invaluable insights about reading people's personalities through well-researched strategies, tried and tested techniques and a bunch of practical tips. These tips can be applied in just about any situation from professional to interpersonal relationships to your social life.

Whether you want to figure out the personality of a prospective buyer during a negotiation or the personality traits of the new date you have your eyes on, this book is a valuable resource for helping you read others effectively. If there's a single largest skill that translates into success in modern times, it is the knack of reading people.

When you know how a person thinks or feels, you can mold your message according to his or her personality for accomplishing an optimally beneficial outcome.

The next step is to use this book and apply it in your everyday life in tiny, gradual ways to start with.

Begin by observing people at the airport, supermarket or doctor's clinic when you have free time. You'll become more interested in the art of analyzing people, and find yourself doing it at every given opportunity.

Finally, if you enjoyed reading the book, please take the time to share your views by posting a review of Amazon. It'd be highly appreciated!

Dark Psychology Secrets

Learn The Trade's Secret Techniques Of Covert Manipulation, Emotional Exploitation, Deception, Hypnotism, Brainwashing, Mind Games And Neurolinguistic Programming

–

Including Case Studies And DIY-Tests

By Patrick Lightman

Introduction

Welcome to the world of Dark Psychology. If you choose to stay, you will find out things you never knew existed. This is a journey not meant for the faint of heart. Secrets of darkness will be revealed, some of which you may find have been used against you.

The good news is that in this book, you will find ways to spot when dark psychology is being used on you or someone you care about. You won't be helpless against the darkness anymore. You will recognize it and know how to deal with it and the person attempting to dish it out.

I've become an expert on this subject due to all the research I've done to understand the powerplay and politics at the top management level of Corporate America. One must delve into the sometimes wicked minds of executives in order to understand them after all. All the better for you that I've found out what lies behind the eyes of what seems to be innocent people.

With my newfound understanding, I found I had quite the different take on individuals I'd just met and even some that I already knew. And you will have this gift too *if* you decide to throw caution to the wind and go down this rabbit hole with me.

Whether you've always been one to see the best in this world or not, you will now find that every person may not be what they seem to be. Many people are out not only to take something from you but to try to keep you down if only to make them stand a little bit taller.

You know the type of person I'm talking about. The ones who seem to rise to the top, even though they've done nothing to deserve it. The people who tend to walk on others to get to the top. If you were aware of what they were trying to do, manipulate you into bowing down, letting them walk on your back, use you as a stepping stone, you would never allow it. These people mask their evil deeds. But soon you will know how to unmask these ruthless individuals. You will have the knowledge to deal with them on their own level.

Or maybe you will prefer not to deal with them at all. Learning how to harness your power and not allow anyone to take it is important too. You too can use dark psychology to help you get to the place you've always dreamt of getting to.

Why can't *you* have the top spot in the company? Why can't *you* have a beautiful home and a fancy car? Why can't *you* figure out how to rise above the crowd to stand out and get what you rightfully deserve?

The answer is simple.

People who know how to use dark psychology have already beaten you to the things you want and deserve. They know they haven't worked for it. They know they shouldn't have it or be in the position they're in. They do not care.

One can look at nearly every politician in office. Many know how to use dark psychology, and they keep using it to stay in positions of power. You see their faces on your television most days on the news. Maybe they're being discredited by others who follow the darkness. Perhaps others are attempting to – for lack of a better word – dethrone them. You won't see them fall, for they too know the secrets and understand how to bend the minds of people. All they have to do is make a select few believe in them, and then they will shake off the attack rather easily.

You, at home, are left wondering how they pulled it off. Soon, you will know how they did it. Soon, you will have the ability to move up if that's what you want to do. Soon, you will have the knowledge that will have you seeing the world in a different light - a light tinged with a darkness that you can learn to see and understand.

It's up to you how you will use this new power. Just remember that with power comes responsibility.

And karma is still a thing that one should watch out for, even if they are using the power of dark psychology.

So, are you ready to take a journey to the dark side?

Chapter 1

Welcome To The Dark Side

Handling Dangerous Knowledge

In this book, you will be given the knowledge that is deemed dangerous. It would be remiss of me if I didn't caution you about the use of anything you find in these pages. Using negativity will only bring negativity upon you. You can understand darkness while not diving into it.

So let's understand what Dark Psychology truly is. It's not an exact science, more of an art form really. It is the study of mind control and manipulation of the mind. Manipulation in various forms is used. Coercion is when one uses threats to force a person into doing things they wouldn't normally do.

Manipulation is the art of making people think they actually want to do or say something that they really don't. Using insidious tactics to turn a person's mind around to benefit themselves is an unfair act that can leave the victim confused. They genuinely don't understand what made them say or do the thing they did. And all the while, the manipulator stands back, mouth closed, and eyes wide open, knowing what they did.

There is the power of persuasion that people using dark psychology can use. Somehow, they say all the right things to make the victim think in the terms they want them too. Gently, they lead the person to say things they wouldn't usually say and do things they never would've done.

And then we have motivation. The old, I'll scratch your back if you scratch mine scenario.

Dark Psychology is used in many ways in our society. I've pointed out how it's used in politics, but what about other places where large groups congregate?

Although it's not usually thought of as a thing that might use darkness to spread the word it's trying to spread; religions can use dark psychology to rein in its congregation. Some top religious authorities use the threat of hell to keep their followers in line.

One might wonder how terrorist groups get any followers at all. When the leaders use all sorts of dark psychology to brainwash people, it gets easier to understand.

Cults gain followers using the same techniques as everything else above does. So, when you get right down to it, wouldn't it be in your best interest to know and understand when someone is using these dark tactics on you or your loved ones?

I know I like the fact that I can easily see through the individuals who think they're so smart and can get anyone to do what they want, evil or not. And when they know that you can see right through them, they typically go away and leave you alone. There's no reason to even attempt to use their tactics on you if you're well aware of what they're doing.

This book is a powerful tool for those who read it. With knowledge, comes power. You will gain insight, you will be intrigued, and ultimately you will see things in black and white and know where you stand and where others do as well. Just make sure you use your new-found knowledge for good, okay?

Beware of the Smiling Guy

Undoubtedly, you've met at least one of these smiling guys who just gives you the creeps right off the bat. Be thankful that you've got that innate sense – some people don't have it at all.

Criminologists and psychologists have something they use to pinpoint people who might have criminal or problematic tendencies. The Dark Triad is a list these professionals can use to gauge the magnitude or depth of the problems a person might have.

Here are the big three:

Narcissism is when a person has a rather massive ego. They boast about even the smallest achievement they've made – or claim to have made. They like to put on airs, also known as being grandiose. This gives them the appearance of being something they aren't. What the outside thinks matters to them a lot. They have no empathy. They don't care to understand where others are coming from or how things hurt them. And one of the craziest things they do is try to get others to empathize with them when they have no empathy for others. This is their world, and everyone in it are merely puppets to them.

Machiavellianism is the practice of deceptive manipulation. They want to use – exploit people to serve them and their missions. They have no moral character nor the morality most people are born with or, at the very least, are taught early on.

Psychopathy is a tricky one. These people can be the most charming people you've ever met. Politicians and religious figures, as well as cult leaders, fit this bill. But that charm isn't always there; it's used as a lure to get the victim into the lair where the person will impose their will on them once they're trapped.

Once they have control over their victims, they will begin to be impulsive. Said with the charm of being spontaneous, these people will impulsively do things without thinking about the outcome, or who might get hurt in the process. That's because they have a selfish streak a mile long. They too have no empathy for others, and what is worse, they don't have a remorseful bone in their bodies.

You have come across people with these three tendencies. There is no way you've lived even a small amount of time and haven't had to deal with one or more people who use darkness to bait you.

There are real-life cases of people who belong in the dark triad, and you meet them all the time. Take this case: I knew a man who hadn't worked but a short amount of time in his lifetime.

How is it that a man who had a wife and children and no disabilities managed to accomplish this feat, you ask? Using dark psychology is how.

He charmed and offered things he could never give, just to get others to put in what they could. Then he used what they'd provided, items intended to help the real unfortunate people he'd claimed he was gathering things for, for himself.

When he'd used up everyone around him, and they no longer would have anything to do with him, he played on the sympathy of his elderly mother. A woman on a fixed income whose husband had died years ago and left her in a home that was paid for, her husband, this man's father, knew he had to set his wife up, or their son would ruin her.

Guess what; he did anyway.

When the world he'd used turned on him, he went to his mother – told her that he was ready to end his life – he had nothing left to live for. His wife and children had turned on him, and now he was on his own.

Of course, no mother wants their child to end their life. So, she did what any parent would and asked what she could do to help. And boy was he ready with a list for her.

'A car, a place to live, three hot meals a day, Mom. That's all I'm asking for,' he pleaded. And she made sure he had those things, giving up her own car to him and giving him a room in her home, plus making meals for her poor, poor son.

One would think that would be enough, but oh no, not for the man who needed it all. Now he just needed to make money. And he couldn't go to work for anyone else because he was so much smarter than everyone else that it drove him crazy to work under people. He needed his own business -nothing big, nothing too expensive. All he needed was 10,000 dollars to make his lifelong dream – a dream his mother had never heard him talk about before – come true. That was all he needed. He could do the rest, and he'd pay her back with interest if that was what she wanted.

'Oh, no son,' she'd said. 'It's a gift to help you get back on your feet. I love you. I want to help you.'

So, he got the money, and for a very short time, he gave this business of his a shot. Not a real shot, a half-hearted shot. And he failed, and he came back to her home. He'd had to sell her car to have enough money to make it back to her home. He was back to square one and just needed a little more help. Maybe the church she used to go to before she got too weak to make it to services would be so kind as to help him.

And this went on and on, for a lifetime. People were used, abused, sucked dry and all for only one man to do nothing more with his life than be the guiltless, immoral, selfish vampire that he was.

At least you have this book. At least you have a way to spot people like this before they ruin your world or the world of someone you love. Because in this book, you will learn how to deal with people like this.

Wired for Deception

The reason the triad of dark personalities even exists in the first place is that we were born hard-wired to listen to what people say and learn as well as develop from what's said. I don't care who you are; you weren't born knowing all you know or acting the way you do now. Your upbringing shaped you, and then you were shaped further by society after getting out into the world on your own.

Not every culture lies to their children, but some do. The myth of Santa and the Easter Bunny are characters that seem so real; children believe them to be true. When you add in that parents use these make-believe characters to get children to act right and be good, or they won't get presents or candy, you've got yourself an example of just how deceptive society is as a whole.

So, don't beat yourself up if you've ever fallen prey to many people out there who are trying to take something from you or have tried to make you see things the way they want you to. We've all fallen victim as well as have played the role of the deceiver in our lifetimes.

Neuro-linguistic programming is a concept that some people came up with in the nineteen-seventies. You have an unconscious mind and a conscious mind. The two don't always seem to be speaking the same language at times.

As the name states, this deals with a person's neurology, linguistics – which is speech, and how to program these things to work for us. If you don't know how to communicate well with yourself, how can you do it with others?

Using NLP – a short term for that long word up there – one can talk to themselves and make themselves understand why we think some of the things we do and how to stop thinking about some of those things.

Here's a little example of how to go about this: I want to stop eating a whole pint of ice cream at a time. I've grown up watching my mother do this, and in my head, I think there has to be nothing wrong with it since she did it. But my weight and blood sugar levels tell me that there is something wrong with what I'm doing. I need to stop. I need to make myself believe that what I've seen from my mother wasn't the truth or right.

I have to have a heart to heart with myself about what is happening and what has happened in the past. I saw something, but that doesn't mean it was right. And this thing I saw may have hurt my mother's health too. She didn't communicate that to me. If she had, I might not have thought of eating all that ice cream at one time was a thing that was okay.

By talking back and forth with myself, I've concluded that my mother didn't think she needed to tell me that eating all that was unhealthy. She had her reasons. Possibly no one had told her about the harmful aspects of what she was doing. Who knows?

The thing is that I had a discussion with myself and taught myself that eating all that ice cream is unhealthy. Now that information is buried in my unconscious mind. And it's in my conscious mind too. So, if things worked right, the next time I go to grab the whole pint out of the fridge, I'll stop, get a bowl and a spoon and serve myself a reasonable amount of the cold, sugary treat.

DIY-awareness tests

Here are a few questions to help you think about what you've just read and learned.

1. If you were told by your parents that there is an Easter Bunny, does this mean you were raised by people with characteristics of the Dark Triad?

_____
_____
_____
_____

_____

2. Can a used car salesperson exhibit characteristics of any of the big three neuroses that make up the Dark Triad? And what are they?

_____
_____
_____
_____

_____

3. Have you been guilty of behaving in any of the ways that were mentioned in this

chapter? And if so, then why do you think you acted that way?

_____
_____
_____
_____
_____

Chapter 2

Manipulation And Emotional Exploitation

Why me?

Why do some people get taken advantage of and others don't? It seems like a crap-shoot, I know. But it's really not.

Everything happens for a reason. If you're gullible, then chances are there is something in your upbringing that made you that way. If you seek approval at all costs, chances are you couldn't find that in your childhood. As sad as it is, what happens to us in our younger years does more to shape us than anything else.

Some children are nurtured. They had stable families with no traumatic upheavals. And they seem to have it all together. Here's the deal; no one has it all together. But some have it more together than others.

If you're frequently the victim of manipulation, then you really need this book. You've got to learn to watch for signs of that whenever you're dealing with authority figures.

You may not fall for it from everyone, but you may have a harder time seeing it in people you're supposed to trust: your boss, your kids, and even your spouse. If people are often trying to sway you to their way of thinking or doing things for them that they should be doing for themselves, then you might have something you should be watching out for.

Here's an example of a person who is being manipulated or emotionally exploited:

Jane goes to work each day. She wants to do a great job and please her boss at all costs. One day, Jane is feeling ill. She's got a terrible headache and calls in to ask her boss for the day off. He tells her he can't spare her today, just come in and do your best.

Sounds reasonable, doesn't it?

Only when Jane gets into work, she finds there are two extra people who've been scheduled to work too. They're actually overstaffed. So, she goes in to tell her boss she really is feeling terrible and since the place is overstaffed, can she please have the day off? She understands she's giving up the pay for that day.

Still, he says he really needs her. She's a great worker. Sorry, she can't leave. And as a matter of fact, she needs to go scrape all the gum off the salesroom floor, and after that, the toilets really need a good scrubbing. And then he needs her to drive downtown to pick up his lunch. He's a diabetic, and this is the only place that has those sugarless twinkies he loves so much. It's his one treat for the entire day; he *so* needs it.

Jane doesn't say what someone who refuses to be emotionally exploited does. She bows her head, tells him she'll do it all and even thanks him before leaving his office.

She could've handled things very differently. She could've done things in a way that would've made her boss see that she wasn't a person who could be taken advantage of nor manipulated. With just a few words said differently, she could've stayed home and taken care of herself.

These words are simple and unfortunately people with the affinity to be emotionally exploited use them far too sparingly.

Here they are – *the magic words*: I'm sick, I won't be coming in today. (There is absolutely no reason to ask a question here. You are sick, and you won't be in – end of subject)

When asked to do something you feel uncomfortable doing, unsafe doing, or that it's not your responsibility to do, here is what you say: No. I will not do that.

When asked why you won't be doing it, here's the magic answer: Because I do not want to.

Now, if you've been giving in to this person for some time, then you can expect some negative feedback. They do think they can manipulate you after all. Don't let them say too much. Cut them off with some quick words of your own. Such as, you have my answer. Goodbye.

It takes practice but staying true to yourself over being true to anyone else is important, and you can do it. The way I think about it is like this. If I'm sick and someone wants to keep pushing me to work anyway, I ask myself, would you die for this SOB? Usually, my answer is no. Now, when it's a helpless little kid or a helpless elderly person, I suck it up and do what needs to be done. Other than that, it can wait, or someone else who isn't feeling sick can do it.

Here are some ways people can manipulate you or emotionally exploit you and how to handle each situation:

Love Flooding

This is when someone is buttering you up to get you to do something that they know you won't want to do. They may come and lather you with affection. Sweet kisses, hugs, nuzzles. "Baby, I love you. Can you get up and do my laundry really quick so I can stay in bed and sleep?"

Normally, you might be nice and do it. But last night you were up with the baby six times. And you've got an appointment with the dentist that you're not looking forward too after lunch. You don't want to get up and even start your day, much less someone else's – even if you truly love that other person.

Here is how you handle this sweet talk but still know that it's a manipulation:

"I love you, but our child kept me up, and I'm not looking forward to my day as it is, so no. You're on your own with your laundry, and as much as I love your affection, I'm not looking for any at this moment. I need my sleep. Night-night."

Lying

Most people can't abide liars – I'm one of those people. I will bend over backward for you, but if I catch you lying to me, then that's over and quick.

Lying happens a lot when someone wants you to give them some money. Here's an example and how you handle it without getting duped.

"I hate to ask, but I don't have a dime to my name, and little Susie has a terrible cold. The medicine is only ten bucks, but I don't have it. If I don't get some money, she'll suffer all night. And I don't get paid until Friday – that's three days away. I'm just worried about Susie is all, or I wouldn't even ask to borrow twenty bucks."

"I thought the medicine was ten dollars?"

"Yeah, it is. But while I'm out, I thought I'd pick up something to eat. You know, hamburgers, fries, a soda or two. Poor Susie is dying for her favorite junk food too. Poor baby."

All of a sudden, you see little Susie running around behind her momma's back, jumping off the furniture, laughing her head off.

Now is your chance to do what's right. So, you say, "She looks fine to me. I would've bought that child's medicine had she been sick. Don't ask me for money anymore." Then walk away without looking back.

Withdrawal

This is a hard one. When someone gives you the cold-shoulder or shuts themselves off to you just because you won't do what they want, then it hurts. I don't care who you are or how tough you might be. When someone turns away from you only because you won't do what they want, it's a terrible manipulation and the epitome of emotional exploitation.

It's easy to say, just don't let them get to you, but man, that's right at impossible. That is until you realize why they're doing it.

They want you to feel terrible for not giving in to them. They want to make you hurt. And for what?

Most of the time, what they wanted doesn't amount to a hill of beans.

Here's an example and how you should handle it:

You come into the living room, your arms full of groceries you need to unpack and put away. Your mother is sitting in the living room, doing her nails. 'Can you run out and feed my dogs, real quick?'

'I can't, Momma. I've got to put these groceries away, and I've got another armload in the car, then I've got to get to the school to pick up Ariel and get her to the doctor to get those warts of hers frozen off. Sorry.'

'My nails are wet. I wouldn't ask you if it wasn't important.'

'I'm sure your dogs won't die before your nails dry, and you can get out there to feed them, Momma. I really am in a huge rush right now.'

'It's just a small favor. You're being selfish. The dogfood is right there by the backdoor. You're right there by it. Now, put one scoop in pen for Fancy and then get a scoop out of the other bag for Bossy, he can't eat what Fancy does.'

'Mom, I know what they eat and how they eat it. I just don't have time right now. If you don't want to go outside, I'll feed them as soon as I get back home."

The bottle of nail polish goes flying. Nothing but the sound of stomping is heard as the room is vacated. The sound of a door slamming is the last thing you hear.

It's not the first time this has happened, and you know it won't be the last. What do you do? The last time she got mad like this, it was three days before she said one word to you?

I've lived this. I've dealt with this over and over on my life. My mother was one person who did this to me and my husband the other. I never learned how to deal with my mother, but you can bet I wasn't going to deal with this from my husband. So, I learned how to handle people who try to manipulate me by using this tactic.

Calmly, you go to where they've shut themselves off from you. You don't have to open the door, just speak calmly through it. "You're upset, that's plain to see. I am busy, that is also plain to see. You can pout, you can keep your distance from me, and you can keep your words to yourself too. You aren't hurting me if that's what you were going for. You're hurting yourself. You deny yourself human interaction." And then you walk away. You don't go do what she wanted you to do, you go on about your business, and if she's still not talking when you get back, you reiterate to yourself that she is only hurting herself, you can't be hurt by that.

Love Denial

Much like Withdrawal, love denial is when a person who loves you holds back that attention because you won't do something, they want you to. You can use the same type of scene from above to deal with that person. You will still talk calmly to them and let them know that what they are doing is only hurting them and not you. They are the ones who are missing out on love and attention by acting the way they are. You have to stay strong here and remain calm. They learned this. It was done to them. Have empathy for that, but don't tolerate it. Don't give in to it. They will learn that at least you won't be manipulated by this action.

Choice Restriction

Many of us have done this with our children. We offer only the choices that we want them to take while ignoring the one we know they really want.

For instance, little Sally is looking at the candy bars in the grocery store. We hold up grapes and apples. "Sally, you get to pick the treat today. Is it going to be apples or grapes?"

With only the two things to pick from, she's stuck.

But that's a child, and you're doing it for good purposes, not evil ones.

Now you're a grown person and you want to eat Chinese for lunch. You and your sister are in the food court at the mall and there are tons of choices. So, it stuns you when your sister says, "Oh, I don't want Chinese today. I'll let you pick though – Pizza or burgers? Go ahead. You get to pick."

I'm pretty sure there aren't lots of you who even need to know what to say here, but I'll put it out there, just in case.

You say, "Get a grip, sis. I'm getting Chinese. You get whatever the heck you want."

Reverse Psychology

Again, many of us have used this method of manipulation on our own children and even grown individuals to get them to see things our way.

You want your kid to put on their protective shoe coverings to go out into the rain. You know that your son hates to be told what to do. So, you say, "It's pouring out, but I don't see any reason for you to put your galoshes on over your new shoes. They should be fine."

"I don't want my shoes to get ruined, Mom. Gee whiz! I'm wearing them today."

You smile, mission accomplished.

But what if it's happening to you?

Your hubby would like his favorite shirt washed but doesn't want to do it himself. He says, "Aw, man. My favorite red shirt is dirty." He grabs up the red shirt and a handful of other clothes out of the hamper. Your white shorts and blouse are in the mix. "I'll just do a load. Don't worry, babe. I've got this."

You might be overlooking the obvious. He's hoping you will see the whites and stop him, take over, do the load yourself.

But you see what he's doing and stop him. "Oh, here let me take those whites. No reason for you to wash these with that red shirt, it'll turn them pink. There you go. You're good to go now, babe."

He's left frowning as his ploy did not work and you walk away with a smile on your face.

Semantic Manipulation

This one is pure torture. I am positive that you've said or been told, "I'm not going to argue semantics with you."

This is when someone wants to use your words, turn them into pretzels, and do their level best to drive you insane.

Think about any argument you've ever had with a child over doing their homework. "But I thought the teacher meant next Tuesday, not today. Why would they expect me to be able to turn it in with only one night to finish it?"

"Um, because it's only three lousy questions that would've only taken you ten minutes to finish."

You're out of your mind, and they're still trying to tell you what they thought.

Although it's nearly impossible to shut this type of thing down quickly, you must try. A calm voice never fails to get someone's attention. "Well, you were wrong about that. So, here it is in nice simple language for you. Do the questions now." Then walk away without saying another word. Don't listen to the rubbish that will surely pour from their lips, just keep on walking.

My best advice to you when you are faced with any type of manipulation at all is to walk away. Sometimes there are no words that will get through to a person. Sometimes you must just remove yourself from the equation.

If words are a thing you find necessary, say them with a calm tone, make it short and concise, and do not expect an answer. Walk away. Leave them on their own to think about what you said or did not say.

Most of all, remember that this is *their* problem, not *yours*. Don't let it become your problem.

DIY Exercises

1. You're busy at work, doing end of the month reports only you can do, when your boss comes in, tells you to put that to side, for now, he needs you to run an errand for him. You can take the reports home to finish them on your own time. What do you tell him?

   _____
   _____
   _____
   _____
   _____
   _____

2. After you tell your husband that you can't stop what you're doing to cut his toenails right that minute, he storms out. What do you do?

   _____
   _____
   _____

3. Your son lies to you about where he was and when you try to get onto him, he yells at you that you lie too. What about the Easter bunny? What do you say?

Chapter 3

How To Sneakily Get What You Want

The power of persuasion is one way to get what you want. And it's not that evil to persuade people to do things, is it?

Advertisements are powerful persuasions. Everyone uses ads to get what they want. Politicians use them, and companies use them. we've even used persuasion to get you to buy this book. So how bad can it be, really?

When used for positive purposes, this power isn't anything bad. But when used for bad things, persuasion can get people into real trouble.

The Power of Positive Persuasion

When a friend has found something new, they really like and want you to join them.

"We went on a trip to the river last summer, Gail. I think you'd love it. You should come with us this year."

"I don't care for water."

"What do you mean, you don't care for water? Everyone loves water. And then there're these gorgeous sunrises and sunsets. You love those."

"I do love those. But the cost is probably much too high for me."

"Is free too high, Gail? I said you could come with us. And there's lots of fun to be had while floating down the river."

"Floating? Oh, no. It sounds dangerous."

"Donny is only five and can't even swim, and he floated down it with us. I think you'll find it safe, fun, and relaxing. Plus, we barbeque each night. You love Allen's ribs, don't you remember?"

"I do love his ribs. How long are we talking about?"

"A week."

"Oh, no. I can't be gone that long. What about my dog, Pookie? What would I do with her while we're gone?"

"She can come too. It's pet-friendly."

"Well, it seems you've persuaded me to go. Thanks, it sounds like it'll be lots of fun."

The Power of Manipulative Persuasion

"Folks, we've got some great deals for you. Step right up and let me tell you all about these steak knives we've got on sale now."

"I have a set already, thanks though."

"No, wait. You don't have *these* knives. These knives are a must for every household. You don't want to be the only guy on your block with cruddy steak knives, now do you?"

"Well, no. But mine are just fine."

"As fine as these. Just look at how they shine. And boy can they cut too. Just look at them slice through this thick steak."

"Well, that's pretty good. They are shiny. But I've got some. See ya."

"Wait. What if I told you that these are the same type of knives they use in the White House? They're good enough for our president and his family and the visitors that go eat with them. So, why aren't they good enough for you?"

"They are good enough for me. I just have some already."

"Why pass up this special offer? You don't know if you'll ever get this chance again. I'm only here for one day. I can't promise you that you'll ever get this chance again. It's the same knives as the White House uses. Don't you want to be a proud American?"

"Oh, heck. Give me a set."

The Power of Helpful Persuasion

"You should totally try this blush, Peggy. It'll look so good on you."

"Um, I haven't ever worn any makeup. I'm not sure how to put it on. I'll just make myself look like a clown if I try to wear any. Thanks though."

"Nonsense, you'd look great with makeup on as long as you don't use too much. I can help you if you want."

"I don't know. I've got this red hair, and my skin is so pale. I've never been able to find anything to match my skin tone."

"You have alabaster skin. It's like God's gift, Peggy. Come on, we can go to the store and I can help you pick out all the right things. For about a hundred bucks, I can get you all set up. And I promise to help you put it on and teach you how to do it so you can do it yourself. What do you say? You wanna let me help you be a better you?"

"Well, when you put it that way, how can I refuse? Thanks."

The Power of Gentle Persuasion

"Good afternoon, Jimmy. How was school today?"

"It was school." He tosses his school books onto the coffee table.

Mom looks at them. "So, do you have homework today?"

"Always," he huffs as he tries to leave the room.

But Mom has something to entice him into doing his homework now, instead of leaving it to the last minute, like he's always done. "I've got some cookies I've just baked. How about I get a plate of them and some nice cold milk and you and I can tackle your homework together? You know, get it out of your way?"

"Not now."

"You don't want any cookies?"

"What? Cookies? You said something about cookies?"

She gets up to go to the kitchen. "Yes, I'm going to get a plate of my freshly baked chocolate chip cookies and a couple of glasses of ice-cold milk. Why don't you take a moment to freshen up, splash some water on your face? I'll take the cookies and milk to the living room while you do that."

"That sounds nice, Mom."

Moments later they meet in the living room. Mom puts the things on the coffee table and picks up one of the books as Jimmy digs into the cookies and milk. "Oh, you have an assignment in biology today?"

"Yeah. It sucks."

"I used to love that class. Care if I take a look at the assignment?"

"Go ahead. Why should I care?"

Flipping to the marked page, she sees the assignment. "Whales, huh. Would you look at this? They live to be over a hundred years old. Can you imagine that?"

"Really?" He sits next to her, looking at the book with her. "How do they know how old a whale can get? Not many people live to be that old."

"Well, let's see." She reads the chapter out loud to Jimmy, who listens intently. And then she asks him the questions at the end of the chapter. "Maybe you should just jot the answers down to save you some time, Jimmy."

"Great idea."

With Mom's gentle persuasion, Jimmy got his homework done.

The Power of Sexual Persuasion

"I really should be going now."

"Why right now? We've got plenty of time."

"My laundry needs doing."

He gently caresses her cheek. "Laundry? I think you'll have time for that tomorrow, won't you? I thought we could open a bottle of wine and sit on the sofa and watch a movie together, just the two of us."

"Well, that does sound nice. But I really should be going. It's getting late."

"My bed has plenty of room if you'd like to stay over." He trails a line of kisses up one side of her neck. "I won't kick you in my sleep, I promise."

"Fluffy probably needs to be let out."

"Don't you have a litter box for your cat?" He snuggles closer to her. "I'm sure she'll be fine until the morning. And it's snowing outside. You really should stay. It wouldn't be hospitable of me at all if I sent you out in this kind of weather."

"I think I'll be fine."

"I can light the fireplace." Another trail of kisses flows over her face. "You'll be nice and warm here, in my arms, in my bed."

"Oh, boy, do you know how to persuade a woman!"

The Power of Bad Persuasion

"I started my diet last night."

"Good for you. Marsha. I wish I could find the self-discipline to start a diet too." Tatum picks up a donut from the box near the coffee pot at work.

Marsha stares at the gooey treat as her friend takes a large bite. "Yeah, I barely have had any cravings at all. So far."

"Wow, how great is that?" The donut drips some red jelly down Tatum's chin. "Oops."

Marsha hands her a napkin. "Here ya go, Tatum."

"Thanks." Tatum wipes her chin. "For lunch, I and some of the other girls from the office are all going to pitch in for pizza. Want to join in on the pizza party?" She puts her hand to her mouth as she raises her brows. "Oh, sorry. I forgot."

"Yeah, my diet doesn't allow pizza." Marsha holds up a brown paper bag. "I brought a salad and some celery sticks from home. Thanks for inviting me though."

Walking to her desk, she pulls a soda out of the drawer as Marsha makes herself a small cup of straight black coffee. "I can't stand that tasteless coffee. I've got to have my soda. I've got an extra can of it in here if you'd like it."

Looking forlornly at the can of soda Tatum shows her, Marsha slowly shakes her head. "It's not on my diet."

"What is on that diet anyway, Marsha? Twigs and berries?"

"Berries? I wish." Marsha sighs heavily. "I should get to work."

A few hours later, Tatum shows up in Marsha's office with one piece of pizza. "I saved you a slice. Come on, one slice of pizza won't hurt you, girl."

"I am starving." Marsha holds out her hand and takes the slice of pizza. "Thanks, Tatum."

Tatum looks at the bottle of water on Marsha's desk. "Here, girl. Have a soda too." She pops it open. "You only live once, right?"

And now Marsha's diet is a thing of the past, just that easily, thanks to Tatum's help and power of persuasion.

The Power of Evil Persuasion

"Look, Joe, everyone is doing it."

"Yeah, but I still don't think I should. My wife and I have a lot of trust in each other."

"She's out of town, Joe. What she doesn't know won't hurt her. Do you know what I'm saying? And that girl hasn't stopped looking at you since we came into this bar."

"Yeah, I shouldn't even still be here. I told my wife I'd get one drink with you guys from work then I'd get home and feed the dog. Butch is probably starving by now. I really should go."

"I ain't trying to be a buttinsky, Joe, but I've seen your wife. She's nice and all, but a little on the plump side and not so easy on the eyes."

"Hey, that's my wife you're talking about!"

"I don't mean no harm, Joe. I'm just saying that you and your wife got married right out of high school, right?"

"Yeah, we were high school sweethearts. She's been the only girl for me."

"Yeah, that's what I'm saying. She's been your only girl. You've got no one to compare her to. And don't even get me started on how boring life would be if all you ever got to eat was vanilla pudding, Joe. And there's a nice cream pie who's just standing there, looking at you, waiting to be tasted. I'm not saying to eat the whole pie, Joe. I'm just saying that you should take a taste of it – of her. What your wife doesn't know won't hurt her, right? Here, have another cocktail to help you get those pesky morals out of your way, Joe."

"Another drink? When did you order this?"

"Just a little while ago. Now that drink cost me five bucks, Joe. I expect you not to waste it. Oh, would you look here? She and her equally as tasty friends are heading our way. I tell you what, Joe. Just to make it easier for you, I'll take her friend. That way you won't be all alone in this. We'll both be doing it. No one will ever know, Joe. No one.

"I'll know."

"Not if I buy you a few more drinks, you won't."

What Would You Do

1. If you were in Joe's situation, what would you do?

2. If you were in Marsha's situation, what would you do?

3. If you were being persuaded to do something you wanted to do but knew that you shouldn't, what would you do?

Chapter 4

Never Buy A Pig In A Poke

Deception is something we have to deal with every day. The old pig in a poke saying refers to the idea that we shouldn't purchase something that we can't see for ourselves. Trusting what someone says about anything isn't always the best practice.

With buying so many things off the internet in recent times, I'm sure everyone has gotten something they didn't intend to get when making purchases off the world wide web.

Even when you buy something at the store that's packaged in a way that you can't see the contents has disappointed most of us at one time or another. With deception being such a huge part of life, what can we do, if anything, to avoid being duped? And how can we stop lying to ourselves?

When We Catch Ourselves Lying

I sat there, watching my coworkers coming into the building I was a security guard at. Being that the company was small, we all knew each other, and most of us got along well.

One by one, everyone trickled into the building to get to their respective offices. When I saw Jennie from accounting getting out of her car in the parking lot, I gasped. She'd not only dyed her hair. She'd gotten it cut too. One of those cuts where half of her head was shaved and the other half was all choppy. And the dye job was something out of a horror movie too – blues and reds and even purples.

For a moment, I had to run through my mind what day it was. April Fools? Halloween?

Nope.

Jennie came in, her lips pressed in a hard line as she looked nervous. "Hi, Amy"

"Hi, Jennie." I tried not to stare or let my mouth agape.

She ran her hand through the side of her hair where she still had some. "I went for a new look."

"I see that."

"It's been a thing I've wanted to do for a while now."

"It has?"

"Yeah. I'm going to audition for a music show next week."

"And you thought this would help?"

"Yeah."

"Oh."

"So, what do you think about it?" She twirled around so I could see the back and I saw that a tic-tac-toe design had been shaved into her hair just above her backbone. "And be honest, please."

Now how in the world could I be honest with this woman?

"Since you're going to be auditioning for that music show, I think you must've done the right thing." *There, that's not too much of a lie.*

"But what do you think about it? Is it a good look for me?"

It's not a good look for anyone.

But I couldn't say that. "Um, yeah. It looks great. You really stand out now, Jennie."

"Thanks. That's exactly what I was going for."

"Well, you've accomplished it alright." So, I couldn't get out of lying to her, sue me!

When We Lie for a Good Reason

"Look, Mom, I know you and Dad never told us about the Easter Bunny or Santa Clause."

"Those are lies, and in our house, we don't tell lies, Sissy."

"I know. But Rob and I want Sam and Lola to get to have those little fantasies that all the other children their age are getting to have. It's not fair for our four-year-olds to be left out of the holidays just because you and Dad don't want to bend the truth a little."

"Bend it? You mean to break it into smithereens, don't you? Or have you forgotten that those things don't exist at all and never have?"

"Mom, please, I really don't want to argue. You are to smile and just nod when the kids talk about the Easter Bunny or Santa. Got it?"

"No way. It's an out and out lie and I won't do it."

"Then I guess you can't ever see your grandchildren until they get too old to believe in those kinds of things. And just so you know, Sam lost a tooth earlier today and the tooth fairy will be paying him a visit tonight after he goes to sleep."

"Why are you doing this to us? All we ever did was be honest with you. What's the big deal? Why can't you just do the same things with your kids that we did with you and your brother?"

"Because my husband got to have Santa and all the rest of the mythical creatures and his childhood sounds like a dream come true to me, Mother! So, what's it going to be? See your grandkids now or wait until they're ten or so?"

"You win, you beast!"

"You mean, the kids win, Mom."

When Lies Sell

I took my sixteen-year-old son to buy his first car. He had five thousand dollars he'd worked hard for and he was ready to make the purchase. We'd come a long way to see a car that a man was selling from his home.

As we pulled up to the place, I had my doubts right away. "I knew it, Timmy. This place is a dump. There's no way this man has a car that's only four-years-old and in pristine condition for what you've got to pay. We should just go and not waste our time."

"Dad, please," Timmy begged with pleading eyes. "Can we just take a look at it?"

I didn't want to disappoint my son, but I knew this man wasn't going to be anything but a snake in the grass. "You'll see, son. Consider this a lesson in deceptive selling practices."

"Maybe it's not, Dad. The picture looked great. You saw it. That mustang looked like it was brand new."

"Yeah, and things in that kind of condition don't ever come so cheap. But you'll see."

We got out and headed to the front door. When a Pitbull came around the corner of the house only to be stopped by the chain he had on, we both came to a stop. "Whoa," Timmy said. "What a dog, huh, Dad?"

I knew there was something not on the up and up with this man and the dog just proved it that much more. "We really should go, son."

The front door opened, and there stood a short man, wearing shorts, no shirt, and sunglasses. "Hey, you must me little Timmy who called about the Mustang. You ready to ride, homeboy?"

"I sure am." Timmy looked around. "Where's the car, Mr. Smith?"

He pointed out back to where a nearly falling down garage stood in the back of the house. "In there. You don't leave something like that out on the street. Let's go take a look at it."

"Can you drive it out here?" I asked as I took hold of my son's arm to stop him from running off after the man, we didn't know at all.

He stopped and looked at me with his head tilted to one side. "Um, no. This way, please."

I made Timmy stay back with me. We barely moved as we followed the man and I whispered, "I really think this is a terrible idea. We should just leave. I can say that I got a phone call and it's an emergency."

"No, Dad. Come on. You're acting like a chicken." Timmy rolled his eyes.

"I'm not a chicken. I'm just not stupid."

The man opened a door on one side of the garage. "Come on. It's in here."

"Why don't you open up the large garaged door?" I asked, warily. "We *will* want to take it for a test drive if he likes it."

"Oh? Well, I can't let you drive it. You can start it and if Timmy wants it, then he can drive it out of here. Once I have the cash in hand."

"Oh, great!" Timmy hurried to go inside the dark garage as I tried to keep up. His eyes were on the prize. "Oh, wow! Look, Dad. It's just like the picture. It's gorgeous!"

I had to admit. There was a car sitting in that dingy, ramshackle garage that matched the picture we'd seen on the texts the man had sent to Timmy. "It certainly looks like the same car."

"Oh, it is the same car," Mr. Smith told me. "It's ready to go too. I've got it all filled up with gas. That way you don't have to stop on your way out of town. You can just get in the car and drive all the way back to your home. Timmy said it was five hours away. Is that right?"

"Yes, that's right." I had the feeling something wasn't exactly right with the car. "And you only want five thousand dollars for this car? Can I ask why the low price? What's wrong with it?"

"Nothing is wrong with it." He ran his hand over the shiny black paint. "It's a beauty. And I just want to give this kid a great deal on his first car. He told me how hard he's worked for that money. Normally, I'd charge over ten thousand for a car this nice. But for Timmy, I seemed to have gotten a soft spot in my heart for him."

My son jumped into the driver's seat then got back out. "Um, where's the key?"

"Oh, we lost it. But you can use that screwdriver on the passenger seat to start it up. It runs great. Try it out." The man looked at me as he shrugged. "My wife, she's no good with small items. She lost them all the time. She lost the keys this morning."

"Dad, how do I do this?" my son called out as he attempted to understand how the screwdriver could start the car.

"Timmy, get out of the car, son." I looked at the man who was trying to sell my kid an obviously stolen car. "Look, you're not dealing with some idiot here. This is a stolen car. We'll be on our way."

Timmy was suddenly at my side. Clutching my arm as he pleaded, "No, Dad! Please. What's wrong? We can get another key. Please!"

"The car's not stolen," Mr. Smith assured me. "I swear."

"Dad, please!" Timmy cried. "This car is like a dream come true for me."

"I've got a deal for you, Timmy. If Mr. Smith has no problem with me giving the local police station a call to see if they can send an officer over here to run the VIN number and make sure this car isn't stolen first, then I'll let you buy it."

Mr. Smith went pale. "Um, see I don't get along with some of the officers on our local police force. But my cousin is a security guard. How about if he okays the car?"

Timmy broke into a smile. "Sounds good to me, Mr. Smith. I trust you one hundred percent."

"I don't. No cop, no car." I crossed my arms over my chest. "Do we have a deal?"

The man shook his head. "Sorry. No deal."

I took hold of my son's arm as he drags his feet. "Come on, Timmy. This isn't the car for you."

"But, Dad."

I leaned in close to whisper, "It's stolen, son."

"I don't even care," Timmy said.

"So, you would give this man your hard-earned money just to drive this car until the police found out it was stolen and came to take it from you to give back to the rightful owner?"

"What if they never found out?" Timmy winked at me. "I won't tell if you don't."

"Get your hind end into my car. We're going to have a very long talk on the five-hour trip home, boy!"

When Lies Hurt

"So, tell me why you said it then if you never meant it?"

"I'm sorry, I really am. I just felt like I had to say it. You'd said it, so I felt like I needed to say it back to you."

"Even though it was a lie? Didn't you think that I would figure out that you didn't really love me? Especially when I saw you with that other man?"

"I don't know what I was thinking. I never meant to hurt you."

"Well, it does hurt. You told me that you loved me. I believed you. I went and bought you an engagement ring. That's how much I believed you. I was ready to marry you."

"I didn't know that. I wouldn't have said yes to a marriage proposal."

"Sure. You'd just lie to me about loving me. I get it."

"I never meant to hurt you."

"It doesn't matter how many times you say that. It still hurts."

When Lies Make You Laugh

I came into the kitchen to find my three-year-old daughter with chocolate all over her face. "Della, did you get into the chocolate cake that I have in the refrigerator?"

"No, Mommy. You said not to, so I didn't get into it."

I opened the fridge to find the cake now on the bottom shelf and a whole handful had been taken out of it. "Well, did you happen to see who stuck their hand in the cake and who also moved it off the shelf I had it on?"

"Um," she swayed back and forth, oblivious to the chocolate cake left on her face and hands. "Maybe a robber did that."

"You think someone broke into our house and robbed us of a handful of chocolate cake?"

She nodded. "Uh, huh."

"I guess I should call the police."

"Yeah, you should cause that's not right to steal someone's cake."

"Can you describe the person who came in and took the cake?" I asked her as I took out my phone.

"Yes, I think it was a tall man with a mustache and some suspenders that looked like rainbows."

"Really?" I tried not to laugh. "And what should I tell the police about why you have chocolate cake on *your* face and hands? And what about those handprints on the fridge too? They're small, just like *your* hands are."

She looked at the chocolatey prints on the fridge she'd just seemed to notice. "Oh, those. Yeah, he had tiny hands too."

"And *your* face and hands?" I asked. "How did *they* get the stolen cake on them?"

"Well, Mommy. It was really sad. He threw the handful of cake at me. It hit me in the face, and I had to use my hands to wipe it off."

"So, this robber broke into our house, and he stole some cake. And he did that just so he could throw it at you?" I had to struggle to keep the smile off my face as she was dead serious.

She shrugged. "I guess he has some issues, Mommy."

That was it. I broke into laughter as she just stared at me like I was insane.

When Lies are Devastating

"So, where were you then, Joe?"

"I was at the bar. I told you that."

"I mean the rest of the night, Joe. You didn't spend the night at the bar."

"Look, I got drunk and slept in my car, okay? I didn't want to tell you that. I didn't want to admit to doing that. You were out of town on that business trip and I was out with the guys from work for the first time since I started working there. And one thing led to another and I had too much to drink. You know I don't ever drink. I think I only had three or four, but they were too much for me."

"I came home early, Joe. I drove past the bar you said you were going to and there were no cars in the parking lot. I came home and you weren't here."

"Did I say I stayed in the parking lot? No, I did not. I drove a little way. They knew I was too drunk to drive. I pulled into an apartment complex that's not too far from the bar."

"And you want to tell me that you fell asleep in your car? You never got out of it? You never went into anyone's apartment to spend the night?"

"That's right. I fell asleep in my car and when I woke up it was light outside, so I started it and came home."

"You didn't know anyone who lived in that apartment complex, Joe? Not a woman named Natasha?"

"No. I don't know anyone named Natasha? I did what I said, and I don't appreciate getting treated like this."

"Like what, Joe?"

"Like a liar."

"See, here's the thing, Joe. Our marriage is on the line here. Do you realize that?"

"I don't see why it would be. I was out, had too much to drink, then slept in my car. There's nothing to divorce over."

"If you had done that, then you are right, there would be nothing to divorce over. But you're lying to me, Joe. To add to the humiliation and betrayal of what you've done to me, now you want to stand here and lie to my face."

"What makes you think that I'm lying to you? What makes you think that I would do anything to jeopardize our marriage?"

"My best friend lives next door to Natasha, Joe. When I got home and couldn't find you, I saw a text that I hadn't noticed that had come in from her earlier in the night. She asked me if I was aware that you and another man wearing a suit and tie just like you were visiting the girls who live next door to her. I was not aware of that. So, I called her up and guess what, Joe? She was still up. Want to know why?"

"Not really."

"Well, I'm going to tell you anyway. She was up because the noise from her next-door neighbors and their guests was so loud, she could not sleep. She told me I should come over."

"So, you went to her place last night after you got home?"

"I did. I went over to her place and I saw your car parked in front of Natasha's apartment, Joe. I looked in your car to make sure you weren't there. I used the key I have to it and unlocked it, opened it up so I could be sure you weren't in it anywhere, not even in the trunk. I wanted to be thorough, Joe."

"And you're sure that was *my* car?"

"My key worked on it. Yes, I am sure it was *your* car. Your blue suit jacket had been left on the passenger seat. Red lipstick stained the collar."

"I don't recall any of that."

"Do you recall a woman screaming your name in the throes of passion over and over, Joe?"

"I do not recall anything like that, no."

I had no choice. I picked up my cell phone, showed him the picture of his car, showed him the picture of him leaving the apartment in the sun's early morning light. And then I let him hear the recording I'd made. "Get out, Joe. Our marriage is over."

When We Have to Lie

My husband came to me one day after work. He looked worried, nervous, and very anxious. "You look awful. What's going on?"

"Where are the kids?"

"Playing with the neighbor kids next door. Why?"

"They can't hear what I've got to tell you. No one can."

I wasn't sure I wanted to hear what he had to say. "Although I'm probably going to regret hearing it, what is it?" I figured it couldn't be that bad.

"I had an accident today." He ran his hand over his face. "My car's totaled."

My heart raced. "What do you mean? How can that be? Why didn't you call me?"

"I couldn't call you. I didn't *need* to call you. It was taken care of."

"How?" I was lost.

"I'm not who I've said I am. And things have changed. We've got to move."

He was acting nuts, talking crazy. Maybe he'd hit his head in the accident or something. "I don't understand." I wasn't taking the kids and moving. I wasn't going to listen to his crazy talk.

He grabbed me by my arms, holding me tight. "I'm not able to stay here anymore. You and the kids have to come with me. It's a matter of life and death."

The doorbell rang and panic filled my husband's eyes. "Why do you look like that?"

"You can't tell anyone that I'm here. You haven't heard from me. Got it?"

"Why?

"There's no time to explain. You don't know where I am. If they ask you to call me, then do it. I won't answer and you will just stick to your story. You haven't heard from me since I left for work this morning."

"I won't lie to the police. If you hurt someone in that accident, then you have to face what you've done." I wasn't going to let him hide from what he'd done.

"It's not the police. It's the mafia. Now do as I've told you too, or they will kill me, then you, and then they will kill our children."

I couldn't believe him. I walked to the door as he went to hide in the cellar. Three men in black suits stood at my door. One of them asked, "Is your husband around?"

"No, I haven't heard from him since he left for work this morning."

Exercises in Morality

1. You hit a car in the parking lot of a large grocery store. No one saw you do it. You look around and there are no cameras. What do you do?

_____
_____
_____
_____

_____

_____

2. One night you're out with friends, drink a bit too much and end up kissing a coworker that your husband has always accused you of having a thing for. Do you tell him what you've done?

_____

_____

_____

_____

_____

_____

3. Your sister comes to see you. She's gained a lot of weight since you've seen her last. She tells you that you look great and asks how she looks. What do you say?

Chapter 5

Covert Takeovers

Covert hypnosis might sound like something that just wouldn't work. After all, a person has to be aware of things if they are going to be hypnotized. The back and forth action of an old pocket watch repeated words. You're getting sleepy. Those kinds of things can't be done without the subject knowing what you're trying to do.

Earlier we talked about NLP. Some of the people who practice this claim to be able to contact the unconscious mind of others. Manipulating thoughts of others without others being aware of what they are doing is what covert hypnosis is.

Of course, with something this sinister, there are huge controversies surrounding the subject. But I'm not here to debate things. I'm here to give you some ideas on how covert hypnosis could work. Then you can decide if it's real or made up just to scare people.

Using Sleep Deprivation to get People to do What You Want

Who of us hasn't ever been sleep deprived? I know I have, and I know my brain felt like cold Jell-O inside my head. Whatever anyone told me I'd done, I simply agreed.

I'd spent a sleepless night with a sick baby. Just as I would doze off, there would go the crying again. I'd get up, walk with him, sit and rock with him, and nothing would work. So, I ended up in the living room, walking, rocking, and watching television just to try to keep my eyes open.

Morning came, everyone else got up and my husband came to me with the television remote in his hand. "Found this in the fridge next to the butter. Care to explain?"

"I didn't do it." I had no recollection of even going to the kitchen, much less carrying the remote and putting it in the fridge.

"No one else was up. You and little John were the only ones. I don't think our six-month-old did it." He laughed. "It's okay. You were out of it. Still are by the looks of things." He gestured to my bathrobe that hung off my nearly naked body. "I'll take him, and you go take a shower."

Glad to hand the baby over, I went to the shower and while under the hot water, I really tried to recall when I had put the remote in the fridge. I had no recollection what-so-ever of doing it.

My job as a detective had me thinking I might try this on some of my perps to get them to admit to things they'd done. So, I took on my first perp that next week.

He'd been brought in on suspicion of human trafficking. I really wanted to get him. So, I had him brought into an interrogation room. And there I let him sit for three hours. Every time he laid his head down, I had an officer go in and wake him up, telling him I was on my way and would be there soon.

Once I saw the signs of fatigue, the drooping eyes, the glazed look, the body that slumped and couldn't sit up straight no matter what, I went in. "Hi. Sorry for the wait."

"Yeah. It's been a while. And this wooden chair ain't all that comfy."

"Yes, I know. I apologize. I just had lots to take care of. So, I'll make this quick. You were found with some items, rope, zip-ties, duct tape, and even some chloroform."

"Yeah, me and my girlfriend like to get kinky."

"Is that so?"

"Yeah. So, can I go now?"

"Not yet." I tapped on the desk, nice and slow, repetitive. I watched out of the corner of my eye as his eyes got droopier and droopier. "What did you say your girlfriend's name was again?"

"Um, I think I said Rosa."

He hadn't even been asked that question. "Yeah, Rosa." I jotted that down, still tapping the desk in the same fashion. "And you bought that stuff we found in your trunk at the Fastbreak?"

"Um, if that's what I said, yeah."

"Did I ask you that?" I kept tapping.

"Didn't you?"

"Hmm, I can't recall. But you did buy that stuff at Fastbreak." I wrote that down. "At noon earlier today."

"Yeah." He looked down at the table. "Or no. No, I didn't do that. I didn't buy that stuff there. I bought it online."

I smiled, happy to have him telling me some truths. "No, you said you bought it at Fastbreak, I asked you about that when I first came in. Don't you remember that?"

"Oh, yeah. Sure."

Waiting a moment, I asked, "And you said your girlfriend is Sally?"

He nodded. "Yeah."

I had him right where I wanted him. "So that is Sally that was in the car with you when you were picked up?"

"Sure. Sally."

"And she was in, on the whole, playing Mr. Grey thing?"

"Yeah?"

"Then why did she run when the cops showed up?"

"I told her to."

"Why?"

"So, she wouldn't talk."

"And why didn't you want her to talk?"

"You know."

"Oh, yeah. Because of what you said earlier."

"What did I say earlier?"

"How she and you were looking for girls to add to your party. You know, as you said, you wanted to show them a good time too and how fun it is to pick up random women who don't know a thing. They're scared at first, but then they get into it and before they know it, they like doing it and it doesn't bother them at all that men pay you so they can do with them whatever they want."

"Yeah, and they get a room and food too. Like, they're winning, ya know?"

"Sure. They get a job and you get money too. A win-win, right?"

He nodded. "Sure. A win-win. I find them on the street or in a club and they get a new life. They love it."

"And you said you keep them at the Shady motel, right?"

"Did I say that?" He shook his head. "I'm beaten. I messed up. I meant the Limelight motel."

I knew I had used some serious mind games on the man, and I knew we were about to find some missing girls and put this man away for a long time.

Playing on Old Fears to get People to do What You Want

I know this wasn't the right thing to do. I had come in late, knew the rules about my curfew, and knew I couldn't get grounded for the week. I had other things to do. Important things. So, I did what I had to do to stay out of trouble.

Curfew was two a.m. I was pulling into our driveway at four a.m., two hours late. My mother was already up, drinking coffee in the living room. She'd turned on the overhead light in the living room, and the porch light too. She was ready and waiting for me to arrive.

I knew I was in for it - and big time. So, what could I do to circumvent the consequences of my actions?

Lie?

Bring up ancient fears in my mother?

Win?

With it still being dark outside, I had that to my advantage. Unseen monsters could still be lurking around that my mother wouldn't be able to see. And with her active imagination and penchant for freaking out over the smallest of things, I used what I knew to my advantage.

Getting out of the car, racing to the front door, I rushed inside, closing the door behind me. "Oh, my God! Did you see it, Mom?"

With my frightened demeanor, my mother already looked a little worried. "What are you talking about? I didn't see anything. Do you know what time it is?"

"Mom, you didn't see that black dog? I think it might've been that stray lab that we saw a few days ago. Remember, it was lurking around in the brush down the street? Mom, it jumped out at the car when I drove by it. I didn't see it at first and nearly hit it. But I managed to miss it. But then it chased me. I'd slowed way down so I wouldn't hit it and that dog was biting at my taillights. Mom, it wouldn't stop barking and growling and biting at the car. And it wouldn't stop chasing me.

"Oh, Lord!" She jumped up and went to look out the window. "I don't see anything. Did it damage the car?"

"I don't really know for sure. It was biting at the bumper and the tires." I recalled an old story my mother had told me about seeing a dog with rabies when she was a kid. "Mom, I think it was foaming at the mouth."

"No!" She locked the door. "Maybe it has gotten rabies and gone mad."

"Yeah, that's what I was thinking." I went to get myself a bottle of water and acted like I was trying to calm down. "Man, that was really scary."

"Oh, I know. I'm shocked that you got out of the car." She kept looking out the window. "I just hope it hears something else and runs off. Dogs with rabies just go after the next thing making noise. It drives them nuts when they hear anything. That's why it bit at the car and wouldn't leave it alone. And had you made enough noise. It would've taken off after you."

"I was being as quiet as I could when I got out of the car. I made sure I didn't see it, but I think I heard it still biting at the bumper." I sat on the sofa, pulling the blanket off the back of it and propping my head on the armrest. "I better sleep in here with you, just in case you see it. I won't be able to rest if I think you might actually go out there and try to kill it."

"No, I'll call the police if I see it. They'll come to take care of it." She sat back down, picking up her coffee cup with shaking hands. "But I'd rather you be in here anyway. I heard a story once about a rabid dog who jumped through a window. The windows in your bedroom go almost all the way to the floor. You get some sleep. I'll keep a watch out for it. Poor dog. I feel terrible about it. It's in such pain right now."

"Yeah, it is. Night, Mom."

"Night, sweetie. You just rest now. I know how traumatic that must have been for you."

"Thanks, Mom. I love you."

Mission accomplished.

Using Panic to make People do What You Want

Case-study: The perp used panic to incite a mass evacuation from the Center for Performing Arts.

The night was calm. A string quartet played softly as the nearly filled stadium of people hummed along. The scene, one of serenity. So, what could possibly happen to get all of these people to scramble to anywhere but inside the safety of that building?

And more importantly, why would anybody want to do such a thing?

I had a lot of questions and no answers. But I was going to get to the bottom of things.

Thankfully, I had the woman who had pulled off the terrible feat in custody. She was tired and willing to talk, finally.

All of five feet tall, the small woman didn't look like someone who went around creating mass chaos on the regular. "So, tell me why you did it, Tiffany."

"He left me." She stared at the floor. "He'd told me I was nothing but a fly on the wall. Too quiet. Too small. Too useless."

"He? Who is he?"

The young, maybe thirtyish, plain woman, with hair cut in a pageboy fashion, wasn't much to look at. She did kind of fade into the woodwork – and it seemed that she designed her look to do just that. "He. My first boyfriend. When we first met, he said he liked how quiet I was. He said he was done with flamboyant women who caused big scenes. He liked me for who and what I was."

"But then he left you and said unkind things to you before he did that." I knew that could really hurt a person. But why go out and try to get others to hurt themselves? "How long ago did he leave you, Tiffany?"

"A month ago." Her red-rimmed eyes slowly came up to meet mine. "Yesterday, I saw him and his new girlfriend. I accidentally bumped into him at the park. She told me off."

"His new girlfriend told you off yesterday?" I could see how that would ignite a fire in anyone.

"She's like almost six feet tall. And really loud and obnoxious. She told me ugly things - things about my height. She called me a troll." She had to stop and sigh.

"Well, you know you're not a troll. You're a beautiful young woman, Tiffany." I always tried to make anyone I talked to feel better. "So, what you're telling me is that she upset you. She upset you so much that you felt you had to do something big. Is that right?"

Nodding, she went on, "She poked me in the shoulder, then pushed me down. And he just watched her do it to me. She told me I couldn't do a thing to her. She told me that the man I had once loved was done with me. He had her now and he was so happy. He'd been miserable with me, is what she said. And when I looked into his eyes, he nodded. Then he finally said something to me."

"And what was that?"

"He told me that I would never amount to anything and that no one would ever even know so much as my name. Well, they will now, won't they?"

"Yes, they will. Only because you're going to go to prison for what you did, Tiffany."

"So." Her eyes went back to the floor. "I don't care. At least those two will have to see my face on the television. They will hear my name. Everyone will."

I had one more thing I had to know. "Tiffany, seeing as you've confessed to this crime. I'd like it if you would tell me how you got all of those people to run out of that building."

"Easy." A slight smile curled her lips. "I started that panic with one word. Bomb. I was in the bathroom, and there were other women in there too. I came out of the stall, acting freaked out and pointed at the empty stall as if something were really in it. Then I shouted with panic in my voice, 'Bomb!' They all ran, screaming, shouting the word, bomb, over and over again. I made them all say the same word. I made them all run. *I* did that. *Me*. Little, old *me*. See, I can make things happen when I really want to, can't I?"

Using Threats to get People to do What You Want

"Dolly, can you run to the bank for me? I need this check deposited this afternoon and I won't be able to take off from work until after lunch."

"Sure." I got up from my desk and went to get the check from my coworker. "While I'm out, you want a coffee?"

"That would be awesome. You're a doll, Dolly."

Nancy always said that little phrase. "Thank you." I never got tired of hearing it either. I liked to be of help to others.

I'd had a tough childhood. My parents had died in a car crash when I was ten. There were no relatives to take me in, so I was put into foster care. Passed from one family to another, I felt left out a lot. And I had to put up with being picked on most of the time too.

Now that I was grown, living on my own, I made it my goal in life to help others to try to put a good spin on my bad past. I'd said to myself that I wouldn't let all that negative rub off on me. I would show the world that one could go through adversity when young and still come out without being broken.

The bank wasn't too far from the building I worked as an administrative assistant in. I walked the five blocks to put my coworker's check in the bank. The company I worked for used the same bank as my coworker did. Making weekly deposits for my employer had me knowing pretty much all of the bank tellers by name and they knew mine too.

The bank was busy, as it was a Friday. I got in line at the back and waited patiently. When the door opened only a few seconds later, I felt a chill run through me. Then a man came up behind me – way too close. I tried to take a step forward to give us more space, but I found him grabbing my arm, then felt something against my back.

His words came out quietly near my ear, "Just be calm and quiet and you won't get hurt."

Panic filled me, but the thing I instinctively knew was that a gun was pressed against my back and I wasn't going to do anything to get myself a shot. "I'll do anything you want, just please don't hurt me or anyone else."

"Don't worry. As long as you do as I say, I won't hurt you or anyone else. But you've got to do everything I tell you to, or I won't only kill you. "He jerked his head at a little girl who was sitting in the common area alone, waiting on one of her parents to get through with their banking business." I'll kill that little girl too."

My heart stopped. "No." I knew he must have something horrible he wanted me to do.

"Yes." He slipped something into my hand. "Give the teller this note when they call you up. I'm going to be right there, sitting right across from that little girl while you take care of my business for me. There's a girl sitting in a black Mustang at the far-left corner of the bank. You take what the teller gives you and toss it into the passenger window of that car. It will be rolled down. From there, you take off, running through the back parking lot."

"They know me here."

"That doesn't matter to me at all. You just do what I say, and everyone will leave here alive. If you don't, then even if I miss hitting you, I *will* hit that little girl."

I was next in line as he left me, going to take a seat right across from that little girl. My mind raced with what else I could do besides rob the bank. I wasn't sure if I would go to jail over that or not. I knew if anything happened to that little girl, I would most likely want to kill myself.

My turn came. Annette smiled at me. "Hi, Dolly. How can I help you today?"

I held the paper in one hand and the check to deposit in the other. "Um, I've got a check to deposit." I slid the check and the deposit slip to her then waited as she did the transaction.

"It's nice outside today. Did you walk over?" she asked.

"I did walk over." I cut my eyes to find the little girl was still there, playing on a cellphone, unaware that the man who sat only four feet away from her could kill her at any second.

"Well, that's it. Here's the receipt, Dolly."

I took it, put it in my pocket then breathed in nice and deep. "I've got this for you too, Annette." I put the note on the counter.

She looked at it, then slipped it under her computer. "Oh, I see. Okay. Let me handle that for you." I watched as she hit the panic button just underneath the counter. "Are hundreds fine, Dolly?"

"Yes." I hadn't read the note. I had no idea what amount of money I was robbing from that bank. All I knew was that I was saving a life."

"I'll put this in an envelope for you, Dolly." Annette looked at me, dipping her head to get me to look at her. "Fifty-thousand dollars? That's right?"

I nodded. "Yes."

She smiled. "Dolly, it's going to be okay." She barely cut her eyes to the man who sat in the common area. "Do what you were told to do. Everything's going to be okay."

I nodded as I took the money then tried not to run out of the bank in a panic. I saw the car he'd told me about and went as calmly as I could to it, then tossed the envelope full of hundreds into the open passenger window. The woman driving, backed out then drove off.

I didn't run, I waited, hiding in the bushes near the place I knew the man would walk out. When he came out, I stopped breathing as he got into another car then drove away.

I wasn't leaving, didn't want to. I would wait for the police. A moment later, the little girl and her mother came out. I finally left my hiding place in the bushes. "Excuse me," I said.

The mother stopped as the child kept walking to the car. "I did it for her. If anyone asks you. If anything happens to me. I did it so your daughter wouldn't be shot."

"What?" she looked confused. The sounds of sirens came floating on the summer breeze.

"I did it for her. I robbed the bank for her."

"Get into the car, Jackie," the woman screamed.

The police cars came screeching into the parking lot. One of them was going so fast. They couldn't stop in time. The little girl was in the middle of the parking lot. "No!"

I stumbled back. My mind numb – I couldn't take it all in. "I did it for her! All for her! Why?"

The girl's mother rushed to her daughter, but it was too late. The police car had run right over her – the officer had never seen her as he was looking directly at me.

One day later, I couldn't take it anymore. That's why I left this note, to let everyone know why I robbed that bank and why I took my own life, twenty-four hours later.

Using Confusion to get People to do What You Want

As I sat in the back of the police car, a warm blanket wrapped around me, I knew I would be okay now. It was all over.

An officer got into the front seat, closing the door. "It's cold out there. We'll be out of here soon. Don't worry. We've got him. And the rest of the girls too."

"Good." I pulled the blanket around my scantily clad body a bit tighter. "My family must be worried sick about me. I've lost track of time. I don't know how long he had me."

"Your parents came in to tell the police that you had been missing since April second. That's eight months, Stacy."

"Wow." Eight months had passed, and I was barely aware of that.

"How'd he do it, Stacy?" the cop asked me. "How'd he get you to go with him?"

It didn't seem real that I fell for it all. But I had. "I was walking out of a grocery store. It was about nine at night. I'd picked up a frozen pizza to make at home. My shift had just gotten over. I worked there."

"Yeah, we know you worked at the grocery store. We know that a man came up to you and you two talked. Then you went with the man." He shook his head as if he couldn't believe it. "Why would you go with a strange man, Stacy? Your parents said it's not like you at all to go off with strangers."

"He was convincing." I shook as I recalled the exact words.

"Hey, lady. You work here?" a man asked me as I came out of the grocery store, I worked at.

"Yes, I work here. What can I help you with?" Even off the clock, I was still an employee at heart.

"I'm having trouble with my car," he said.

"Oh, I'll go back inside and ask one of the guys to help you out. I don't know a thing about cars. Sorry." I stopped to go back inside to see if I could get some man to help the guy.

"That would be awesome." He reached out and touched my arm, halting my actions. "But I've got this baby girl with me and she's crying like crazy too. My wife, her momma, is back home and I don't know what to do. Maybe you could sit in the car with her while I go inside and find another guy to help me out. Do you think you could that for me?"

Something told me not to do it. I felt a rush of cold move through my body. "Oh, I'm not sure."

All of a sudden, the man's cell phone went off. "Shit!" The ringtone was kind of odd, chaotic, and loud. I froze as he took the phone out of his pocket. "Honey, I'm trying to hurry." I could hear someone crying on the other end of the line. "Baby, I know you're sick. I'm trying to get the medicine. I'll be back as soon as I can. The damn car broke down on me." More crying and shouting at the other end of the line, then he said, "I'm sorry! I'm trying! I just need help."

"I'll go sit with the baby," I offered as the man seemed to be on the verge of tears and the woman on the phone was already in tears. I had no idea what was going on in their lives, but it sounded tragic. "Show me where the car is."

"Thank you. You're an angel sent from above." He walked toward the back of the parking lot and I walked along beside him. "Honey, this nice lady is helping now. I'm sure we'll be home soon. Try to rest until we get there. I love you, babe." He ended the call and put the phone back into his jeans pocket.

"Wow, it sounds like you all are having a really hard time." I saw the hood open on the one car parked in the back row. "What's wrong with the car? It just won't start or what?"

"Yeah, it won't start is all." He stopped at the back of the car. "Thanks a lot. We are having a really hard time. You can get into the back seat there. Little Lila is in her car seat. It's quiet. Sounds like she might've fallen asleep, thank the lord above. If you'll just get in and sit there in case she wakes up. I'll run back in and get some help."

"Sure. No problem at all." I opened the back passenger side door and saw an infant's car seat on the other side of the car. A baby, or what looked like one in the dark, was all bundled up inside of it. I got in, closing the door behind me to keep the cool night air out.

When the hood slammed shut, I jerked my head up to find the man had closed it and was getting inside the car, behind the wheel. I had no idea what was going on and tried to open my door, but it wouldn't open. I jumped over the baby and tried to open that door, but it wouldn't open either. "Stop! Let me out!"

The soft blankets where the baby should've been smelled weird. I pushed the blankets and found nothing was in them and the man wasn't speeding away but driving a normal speed to be leaving the parking lot. "Just go to sleep," the man told me.

My eyes were getting heavy and I had no idea why that was. "No. Let me out." I tried to climb over the seat to get out the front passenger door.

He pushed a rag against my face. "Just go to sleep."

I felt it all going black and fell back into the back seat. And that's all I remember about that. When I woke up, I was in a dark room, like a motel room and my clothes were gone, my hands and feet tied to bedposts.

I looked out the window of the squad car, watching another officer take the man who'd lied to me so convincingly and put him in the back of another cop car. "You know, I think I wouldn't have fallen for it if it wasn't for that damn phone call he got. It became so chaotic that I stopped thinking and just tried to solve the problem any way I could."

"Yeah," the officer said. "He pulled covert hypnosis on you. He did it to most all the girls he kidnapped. He used chaos to get you out of your own mind. Then he put into your unconscious mind the need for help and you had no real choice except to help the man. It's a human reaction and he used it against you. It's a pretty damn dark and insidious way to get people to do what you want them to. I wish I could tell you that it would never happen to you again, but I'd be lying. It's actually been proven to work over and over again on the same people."

"No way!"

Let's See What You Think

1. You've read about some pretty dark ways to get people to do what you want them too. Would you stoop to using any of these tactics? And why or why not?

_____

_____

2. A woman comes up to you, crying inconsolably. She keeps trying to get you to come with her, but you're not sure why. It seems important though and she seems so upset that she couldn't actually harm you. Do you go with her to help or do you walk away? Why or why not?

_____
_____
_____
_____
_____

3. You've got a lot on your plate at work. Your boss has given you a strict timeline to get a project done. You will not be able to get it done on time and he's told you that your job is on the line. Do you come up with an elaborate tale to get your boss off your back and get your time extended? Or do you accept the fate of being fired?

_____
_____
_____
_____
_____

Chapter 6

Hostile Mind Takeover

Brainwashing – a scary word. No one wants to believe that they could be brainwashed, but it happens. It happens more than you even know.

Brainwashing is known by other names too – mind abuse, coercive persuasion, and thought control. What happens, is a person or even a group of people use systematic methods to get the victim to bend or conform to things they wouldn't conform to otherwise. Think about members of a cult.

That's scary, but even scarier is the fact that advertisers have learned these dark techniques and use them regularly on the unsuspecting public.

To make this complex subject easier to understand, I've written some life-like scenarios for you.

Only One Conclusion

The day was long, the food supply limited, and picky eaters would prove hard to deal with. I was alone with my two sons in a remote cabin in the woods. Their father had gone out hunting and wouldn't be back for at least two days.

We were on our own with the little we had. My ten and twelve-year-old sons didn't care for much, other than fast food. I had my work cut out for me.

Not young enough to force them to eat what I wanted them to, the boys would have to *want* the food I had to offer.

But how to get pre-teens to think they actually wanted to eat something they'd turned down most of their lives?

"Hey, I was reading the other day how the turkey is a superfood." I brought up.

"Turkey?" Garrett asked as he made a face. My twelve-year-old thought himself a connoisseur of not so fine foods. "If that's such a superfood, then why isn't it sold at any of the places we eat, Mom?"

"Well, grapes are a superfood and you can't get them at the places you eat either." I felt that needed to be pointed out. "And we are out here in the wilderness - twenty miles from any town. If your dad doesn't make it back for any reason, then we'll have to hoof it out of here. And the snow is only getting deeper by the day."

"Are you saying that we should build ourselves up in case we have to walk out of here, Mom?" Bryan, our ten-year-old asked.

I shrugged. "You never know. Might as well be prepared, right?"

My sons looked at each other then Garrett asked, "So, what about this turkey you read about?"

"It's a superfood. It's got protein and other vital nutrients."

"Yeah, and it's gross," Bryan said.

"Do you think that muscle-building protein is gross, Bryan?" I asked.

Garret flexed his tiny bicep. "I'm strong enough."

"Are you?" I looked out the window as the snow fell outside of it. "Are you strong enough to fend off, let's say, a wolfpack?"

Both boys looked a little frightened "Nope," they said.

"Do you think that eating a superfood, like a turkey could help you fight them off if it came to it?" I asked.

Bryan nodded. "Superfood is in the name, so I would think it could help."

"And what about hunger? Walking all that way, twenty miles could deplete your energy. My bets are on that it would. Wouldn't it be best to have fueled your body with the best stuff you could so that you would have stamina much longer than if you'd eaten junk?"

Garret agreed, "Yeah, eating superfoods sounds like the best thing to do if you're faced with something like that."

"Yeah," Bryan agreed.

"So, if you had the choice to eat cheese pizza or a turkey sandwich on whole-grain bread, which would you pick if you had to walk twenty miles in the snow and possibly take on a pack of wolves along the way?"

"Turkey sandwiches!" they both shouted.

"Great." I got up to go make them some. "Since we have no idea what we're in for. Do you boys think tonight's dinner should be some turkey sandwiches or that one frozen cheese pizza we've got?"

"Turkey sandwiches!" they shouted again.

And we have a winner!

The Same Phrase

"My mother had a new friend over the other day and something she said just won't leave my mind," I told my husband. "And Mom has been going to meet with this little church group with this woman for over a week. Now, Mom's saying this thing a lot and I don't know if I like it."

"What is it?" he asked me.

"It seems benign. I know it does, but it's just that her friend said it over and over. And now Mom's doing it." I couldn't shake the feeling that something bad might happen if I didn't tell someone what I'd overheard.

"So, what is it, Beth?" my husband asked, growing impatient.

"The name of the man who heads up this little church group – a group who meets in the member's homes, instead of a real church – is Barney." Even saying his name gave me chills.

"And what does that have to do with what this woman and your mother have been saying?" he asked me, looking aggravated as he rubbed his temples.

"It's his name. The woman kept starting out her sentences with, Barney says. It was odd. She said things like Barney says we should all eat tuna fish. My mother asked her why and I swear to you that the woman merely shrugged and said that she didn't know. No one asks Barney why he says the things he says – that would be rude. Anyway, she went on to say that since she's added tuna to her diet, she feels great."

"That's not so bad," my husband said as he laid back in our bed. "I don't see what you're worried about."

"She said other things too. Like this, Barney said we all need to put ten dollars into the pot each time we meet. And she also said Barney, says we need to meet every other day, so we don't forget the words." I shrugged. "I don't know what she meant by that, but I didn't like it. And I didn't like what I found at Mom's today."

"What did you find in your mother's house?"

"A whole shelf in her pantry is nothing but canned tuna fish. And she's got an envelope from her bank with nothing but ten-dollar bills in it too." I just knew something wasn't right with this little church group. "And she told me that she joined that group and then she said this, Barney says we should all bring at least one new person to our group each month. Barney says when we get one hundred followers that we can buy a place where we all can live. Like a camp. We will all live in one, great big home, and we will all take care of each other for the rest of our lives."

"Great!" my husband said. "I've always worried that your mother would end up living out the remainder of her years with us. Thank goodness she found this group."

"No! I think he's a cult leader or something." I smacked him on the arm. "She said that Barney says they are all going to put all their money into one account that he'll oversee and make sure everyone is taken care of."

"I still don't see a downside," my husband said, then snuggled down and went to sleep.

Too Many Questions

"How would you like it if a man took your wallet, Joey?" he asked me.

"I," I couldn't say anything else as he jumped right back in.

"How would you like it if someone stole your dog, Joey? How would you like it if you stepped on a nail? How would you like it if your mom went to jail? How would you like it if I took your stuffed teddy bear? How would you like it if you couldn't ever drink water again?"

"Stop!" I screamed.

But he didn't stop. "How would you like it if popcorn were no longer available? How would you like it if there wasn't any more snow, Joey? How would you like it if I ran over your toe with my car?"

"I wouldn't like any of those things."

"So, how would you like to go to the movies with me?"

"Movies? Yeah, sure." I hadn't wanted to go anywhere with him, but I'd do anything to shut him up.

When Fear Bends Your Mind

I sat at my desk in my office on the fifth floor when a strange man ran into my office, breathing hard and looking scared to death. "Thank God, I made it." He slammed the door closed behind him, locking it. "There's a fire out there. The whole place is on fire. I'm looking for all the survivors I can find to help them." He came at me quickly, pulling me out of my chair. "You've got to get out of here."

"I don't smell any fire."

"No, it's not quite here yet. But it's coming and it's coming fast. You're going to have to jump."

"I'm on the fifth floor! I can't jump."

"You would rather burn alive?"

"I would *not* rather burn alive."

He pushed me to the window then opened it. The ground looked so far away. "Here you go then, time to jump."

"But," I got up on the ledge. "I don't see any smoke."

"It's billowing out the other side. Hurry, there's no time to waste." He gave me a slight push. "Jump! Now!"

And so, I did and that was when I broke my legs all because of one crazy as sin man.

When Anger Bends Your Mind

"I said no!" she screamed at me.

I hadn't even wanted to drink the beer until she did that. "You aren't the boss of me."

"You will not drink that beer!"

"Um, hell yes I will. You won't tell me what I can and can't do. I am an adult."

"I will make your life a living hell if you drink even one sip of that beer!"

I turned it up and drank it all down. "To hell with you. I do what I want!"

Isolation and Brainwashing

Joe grew up on a remote farm with only his grandparents around. With only the three of them, Joe knew nothing more than what he'd been told his entire life.

When I got out of the car to pick him up and take him with me to a new home, a place where he'd be safe since the death of his grandparents, he tried to run away. "No. I won't go. You're not real!"

I had another caseworker come in from behind the small house. "It's okay. We're here to help you, Joe."

"No!" the fifteen-year-old boy screamed. "There's no one else on this planet. Why would they lie to me? Why?"

Joe was the victim of grandparents who thought it best to keep the boy unaware of outside life. They'd had to raise him from an infant when his mother took off and left him at their home. She was in a cult and they wouldn't let her keep the baby she'd been pregnant with before she joined them.

I had to try to make him understand why people he loved would do such a horrible thing to him, "They did it only because they loved you, Joe. But it was all a lie. Now come with us and everything will be okay. I promise."

He fell to his knees in the dark dirt. "They promised me too, lady. They promised me too!"

Brainwashing in Advertising

I sat there, my toothbrush in hand and the tube of toothpaste that I'd used for years and years in the other. "Nine out of ten dentists recommend this brand, Danny. You should use it too."

"How do you know that's true?" My new boyfriend came to stand at my side. "I use the other brand and guess what?"

"What?" I asked as I began brushing my teeth.

"That commercial says that nine out of ten dentists recommend my brand too. Think you might've been brainwashed?"

Have I?

Some Thought-Provoking Questions

1. For years you've been told that there is no snow on Mount Olympus. Then you see a picture of the mountain on television and see snow on it. How do you feel about that?

   _____
   _____
   _____
   _____
   _____
   _____

2. You go to a meeting with a friend and find the charismatic leader of her group has lots of ideas that are way out of the norm, but he's so cute and he's smiling at you so much. What would you do if he asks you to join the group and leave your family behind?

_____
_____
_____
_____
_____
_____

3. You find a man running into your workplace, screaming that terrorists are coming. You all have to hide. What do you do?

_____
_____
_____
_____

Chapter 7

Playing Games

The art of playing mind games has been practiced throughout history. Here are a few life-like scenes to help you spot them and hopefully help you to know when someone is playing with your mind.

Testing Your Faithfulness

"So, I'm seeing Joey, right," I told my best friend. "And he does this thing last night that totally freaks me out, but like in a good way, I guess."

"What did he do?"

"Well, his best friend called me all late and stuff and he asked me if he could come over. He told me that he really likes me and that Joey never had to find out."

"What did you do?"

"I totally told him that I was with Joey and that he needed to respect his friend a lot more than he was. And then I hung up on him."

"But how was Joey a part of that?"

"Oh, he called me right after and told me that he'd set me up. He gave me a test on faithfulness, and I'd passed. Yeah, me!"

"I think that was a pretty manipulative thing to do. You don't see it that way?"

"No way. It means he loves me."

"Not."

When They Really Want What You Have

"So, girl, I know you're in love and all that, but I saw your man, Tyrone, talking to Sara. Sara from the bar!"

"No way." I felt myself dying inside. "I thought he loved me."

"Yeah, I know right?"

"I don't know what to do."

"Break up with him before he gives you a disease, girl. You know what you got to do. Don't even tell him that you know about what he did. Just tell him that you don't love him anymore. Stick it to him before he can stick it to you."

"You're right. You're a great friend. Thanks, Ruth."

One week later...

Going into the club, I see Ruth sitting on Tyrone's lap. And by the look I found on her face, I think I had been played.

Getting Played Over Food

I sat down at the table in the cafeteria with my plate, hungry and ready to eat. "Boy, I am starving today."

Jane looks at my plate. She has nothing in front of her. "Yuck. That looks nasty. I bet they put dog food in that. That is what it looks like."

"It's chili." I look at the plate full of the food I had thought looked delicious.

"Well, chili or not, it looks like it came out of a can with a dog's face on it." She turns her nose up and looks the other way.

No longer looking at the food the same way, I feel my stomach rumbling for something else. "I'm gonna go get a bag of chips. This does look disgusting." When I come back, the plate is empty. "Um, who ate that nasty stuff, Jane?"

"I did." She wiped her mouth off. "Turned out. It was good after all."

And I ate my stale chips as I kicked myself for falling for that load of bull.

Played for Money

"Momma! Momma!" I walked into the house to see if I could score some cash to go to the movies.

"What?" she called out.

"Momma, I need some money."

"Nope."

I found her on the sofa, watching television. "Please."

"No. You still haven't done the yard work I asked you to do last week. I gave you ten dollars for that before you did the work. I ain't falling for that ploy again."

"All I need is five bucks, Mom. Look, if you give me the five, then I'll not only do the yard work, but I'll sweep and mop the whole house for you tomorrow."

"I don't know. I can't trust you."

"Sure, you can. I promise."

"Well, I guess I can give you one more chance." She takes out a five and gives it to me. "Have fun tonight. Tomorrow though, you got to work."

The next day...

I'm hurrying out the door. "Hey, where are you going? You promised me you'd do the yard and sweep and mop, remember?" Mom asked.

"Aw, man. I forgot that I've got a basketball game, Momma. Sorry, the team needs me. You understand, right? Love you. Got to jet."

I'd had my fingers crossed behind my back when I made that promise anyway!

Played for a Fool

I saw this ad in the paper for a boxer puppy for free and went to see if I could get it. When I came up to the house, I saw an old man sitting on the porch. "Mister, I'm here for that boxer puppy you've got for free."

"Oh, good. I've been needing a good home for my puppy." He got up and went inside then came out with a tiny dog that looked nothing like a boxer. "Here he is."

"Um, it's pretty small." I took the puppy out of his hands.

"He's only six weeks old."

"The ad said you've got papers for him. It said he was registered."

"Oh yeah, I forgot. Let me go get them." He came back with a piece of paper. "Here you go."

The paper looked legit. "You got pics of his parents?"

"Sure do." He pulled out his phone and showed me many photos. "See?"

Nodding, I left with my free registered boxer puppy.

A few months later, when my dog hadn't grown even a little, I took it to the vet to see what was wrong with it. Turned out nothing was wrong with my puppy. It was a full-grown chihuahua. That was all.

Seemed I'd been played for a fool.

What Would You Do

1. You've got to get rid of some kittens. You have to move, and you need them gone to good homes fast. They all have these cool stripes that look a lot like those on a Bobcat. Do you advertise them as a rare breed of cats

called, Manx's and maybe even make a buck or two from them?

_____
_____
_____
_____
_____
_____

2. You want to know if your girl is cheating, so you set her up to see if she'll fall for your friend. Do you feel this is right or wrong? And why?

_____
_____
_____
_____
_____
_____

3. You're starving but you have no money. Your friend has food that you'd love to eat. Do you make it seem unappetizing, so she won't eat?

4. _____
_____
_____
_____
_____
_____

Conclusion

Now some of the things you read in this book were funny and some were sad, while others where scary. All of them played on your emotions. They were meant to make you think.

Life isn't easy, fair, or even right at times. Sometimes it seems there is nothing we can do about it either. But that's not completely true. *You* can make a difference.

It's up to you what you do with what you've learned in this book. My hope is that you don't do anything you've learned in a bad way. But I do hope you learn to recognize when someone is pulling some of this dark stuff on you or someone you care about. You've got the power to turn things around.

Life is unfair, tragic, and full of surprises. What you do with it is all up to you. Make your life count – for the good.

The End

Finally, if you enjoyed this book, then I'd like to ask you for a favor. Would you be kind enough to leave a review for this book on Amazon?

It'd be greatly appreciated!

Thank you and good luck!

www.ingramcontent.com/pod-product-compliance
Lightning Source LLC
Chambersburg PA
CBHW051537020426
42333CB00016B/1972